Point Reyes National Seashore

A Hiking and Nature Guide

Don and Kay Martin
Illustrated by Bob Johnson

Acknowledgments

We are extremely grateful to all of those who have helped and encouraged us in writing this book. At the National Park Service, we thank John Del'Osso, Jack Williams, Bill Michaels and especially Dewey Livingston, who provided valuable historical information and reviewed parts of the manuscript.

A special thanks to those we consulted for natural history information, Geoff Geupel at PRBO, Jim Locke, Al Molina and Joe Mueller at the College of Marin. We are also grateful to Sue Baty from the Jack Mason Museum who provided historical photos and to Stephen Prata and Ted Bright at the College of Marin who provided Macintosh computer support.

We would also like to thank our friends and hiking companions, Dick and Sharon Shlegeris, Bill and Dixie James, Ruth and Steve Nash, Shel and Joy Siewert, Phil and Mary Neff, and especially Jennifer, Theresa, Susan and Greg Martin.

Picture Credits
17 - Bear Valley Country Club: Anne T. Kent California Room, Marin County Library
39 - Bass Lake: photo by the authors
59 - Schooner *Hartwood*: Point Reyes National Seashore
61 - Drakes Monument: photo by the authors
63 - Schooner *Point Reyes:* Point Reyes National Seashore
67 - Tule Elk: photo by John Aho, Point Reyes National Seashore
69 - The Oaks: Jack Mason Museum
90 - Lighthouse: Dewey Livingston, Point Reyes National Seashore
113 - Golden Hind watercolor: artist William Gilkerson, courtesy of National Maritime Museum, SF National Maritime Historic Park
115 - Wreck of the *Samoa:* photo by Mrs. Clarence R. Pape, courtesy National Maritime Museum, SF National Maritime Historic Park
115 - Home Ranch: Jack Mason Museum

Table of Contents

How to Use this Guide
Getting There
Most Frequently Asked Questions
Ticks and Lyme's Disease

How to Use This Guide

This guide book can be used in three ways. First, it can be used at home to plan an outing or hike. Second, the book can be taken along on the hike to read descriptions and maps. You might also pick up a free one-page trail map at the Visitor Center which can be folded to fit into a pocket. Then, you can just refer to the book at major junctions or rest stops. Third, the book can be used as a reference book for identifying birds, animals, flowers and tidepool organisms.

Choosing A Hike or Outing

When planning a hike or outing, the first consideration should be the weather. For example, in summer, the coast is often cold and foggy, especially in the morning. The fog usually clears off by noon, then returns with strong northwest winds in the late afternoon.

Two other factors to consider when choosing a hike are distance and elevation change. If you are new to Point Reyes or new to hiking, it's best to choose a hike conservatively. Three miles of hiking in mountainous terrain can take twice as long and be twice as hard as three miles on flat terrain.

Once you've selected a range of distances and elevations, there are several questions you might consider. What is the best hike for this season? What wildflowers are in bloom? Where are the best view hikes? The best hikes in hot weather? A good place to begin answering these questions is to look at the suggested hikes in Appendix A1 and A2.

Hike Descriptions

If you're wondering how we arrived at the various ratings used in this book, here is a sample entry and brief description of the method used.

Distance: 6.9 miles
Elevation Change: 1300'
Rating: Hiking - 10   Good trails, occasionally steep.
When to Go: Excellent anytime, best from March to June.

Distance

The distance measurements were determined by a combination of methods including information from other books, park maps and trail signs, and measuring distances on maps. Distances between mileage points are probably accurate to 0.1 miles, while overall distances are good to 0.2 miles.

Elevation Change

The elevation change was taken from USGS maps. For hikes that make one long trip up, then down, the elevation change is fairly accurate. A few trails like the Inverness Ridge trail behave like a rollercoaster and elevation information is less accurate.

Rating

The hike rating depends on aesthetics. How interesting is the hike? For example, the Bear Valley - Old Pine - Sky Trails, Hike 3, has interesting flora, varied terrain and good views. We consider it interesting 95-100% of the time and so, rated it a 10. On the other hand, the Coast trail to Double Point, Hike 13, is an out and back hike along roads and, in some areas, has little change in flora. We consider it interesting about 65-70% of the time and rated it a 7.

Obviously, this rating system is subjective and depends on what we like. Also, the rating system is dependent on the season. For example, the same Coast Trail, Hike 13, is far more interesting in the spring when the hills are green and the flowers bloom.

The rating of hikes is based on the best possible conditions, the best season, views, weather and wildflowers.

When To Go

The When to Go rating is based on flora and fauna, weather, season, views, trail and road conditions. Because Point Reyes juts out into the Pacific Ocean, its climate is strongly influenced by marine conditions. Winters provide rainfall, water runoff, migrating birds and whales and often plenty of sun. Spring offers wildflowers and these two seasons are the best times to go on most hikes.

Disclaimer

Trails change, roads change, plants change, trees fall down, signs change and hikes change. In winter, some trails and roads may be impassable. This book is only a guide. We can not accept responsibility for trail conditions or for trail information. Although we have tried to provide the best information possible, there may be typographical and content mistakes. This is our disclaimer that we do not accept liability or legal responsibility for any injuries, damage, loss of direction or time allegedly associated with using this book. To be certain of the best information available, check or call the Bear Valley Visitor Center for trail information. At any given time, a few trails will probably be closed for repairs. For example, the beach access trails at Sculptured Beach and Ocean Beach are often closed because of erosion or from being overgrown with poison oak.

Precautions

Poison oak for some is a minor irritation, for most, a major irritation and for a few, a medical emergency. The best advice is to learn to identify the plant by its leaves and avoid touching it. An old saying is,

> "Leaves of three, leave it be."

In fall, poison oak leaves turn crimson red and drop off. In winter, the bare branches are difficult to identify, yet still retain their toxic oils. It helps to stay on designated trails and to watch out for branches that lean out onto the trail or drape down over the path. Poison oak is very common at Point Reyes.

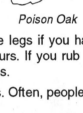

Poison Oak

Stinging nettles also cause skin irritation if touched. Usually, nettles are small and only hit the legs if you have shorts on. The sting will generally last from 2-8 hours. If you rub the sting with an alder leaf, it might relieve the symptoms.

Fluids are essential when hiking or staying outdoors. Often, people go hiking or go to the beach and wind up the day with a mild headache. Usually, this is attributed to too much exposure, too much sun or too much wind. Many times, the problem is too little fluids. Hiking or sitting on the beach requires a minimum of 1/2 quart of fluids per hour, and often more, depending on the temperature and elevation change. Alcohol does not count. It is a diuretic which means that it removes fluid by osmosis in the stomach. It is always a good idea to carry water on a hike and to drink it whether you feel thirsty or not.

Plan to drink 1/2 quart of fluid per hour on hikes and at the beach.

Using The Maps

The detailed 3-dimensional maps show "3-D slices" cut from the Point Reyes peninsula as shown in the figure. The viewing angle is 40 degrees from the vertical and the maps are displayed in orthographic projection. This projection removes perspective and keeps all distances the same. No part of the map is any closer to the observer than any other part.

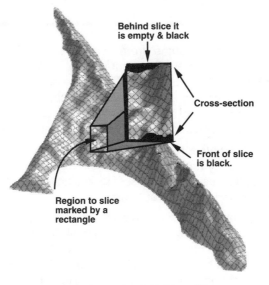

Behind slice it
is empty & black

Cross-section

Front of slice
is black.

Region to slice
marked by a
rectangle

Expanded View of a 3-D Map Slice

Symbols used on these maps include:

📍   Ranger Station and Visitor Center

🚶   Trailhead for each hike

⛺   Backpacking camp

🐎   Stables and horse rentals

Identifying Birds, Flora and Fauna

Each hike includes information about the birds, wildflowers and animals that may be seen. Appendices A8 to A16 provide references to help identify them.

Wildflowers are identified using their common names. Sometimes, we use one common name to refer to more than one species of a flowering plant. For example, there are three species of lupine on Point Reyes, but we do not distinguish between them in the hike description. In the Appendix, we describe just one species of each kind of wildflower.

No matter how you use this book, we hope that you will enjoy Point Reyes as much as we have enjoyed preparing this guide.

Getting There

There are four major routes from Hwy. 101 to the main park headquarters at Bear Valley. The best way to the Visitor Center is to take the Sir Francis Drake turnoff in Greenbrae and stay on it through San Anselmo and Fairfax all the way to Olema, then turn right and take the Bear Valley road the last half mile. This route is 23 miles long, but it takes forty-five minutes to an hour depending on traffic.

The southern alternative route to Bear Valley is to take the Hwy. 1 off-ramp in Mill Valley and follow it north through Stinson Beach. This route is about 28 miles and, while scenic, is significantly more difficult, taking up to one and one-quarter hours.

There are two routes west from the northern section of Hwy. 101. You can take the Lucas Valley Road off-ramp at Marinwood and head west towards Nicasio and Point Reyes Station. Or, if you are further north, you can take the Point Reyes-Petaluma Road. Both of these routes are longer than the Sir Francis Drake route, but they offer pleasant, rural scenery with rolling hills.

How to Get to Trailheads North of Bear Valley

The following trailheads are located along Limantour Road:
- Sky Trailhead - 4.8 miles (all distances are from Bear Valley)
- Bayview Trailhead - 6.0 miles
- Hostel and Muddy Hollow Trailhead - 7.5 miles
- Limantour Beach and Trailhead - 9.1 miles (about 20 minutes)

The following trailheads and points of interest can be reached by taking Sir Francis Drake Hwy. west:
- Estero Trailhead - 10.5 miles
- Point Reyes Beach North and South - 16.4 and 13.8 miles
- Drakes Bay Visitor Center and Trailhead - 16.4 miles
- Chimney Rock Trailhead - 20.3 miles
- Lighthouse and Visitor Center - 20.4 miles (about 40 minutes)

The following points can be reached by taking Sir Francis Drake Hwy. to Pierce Point Road and then heading north:
- Tomales Bay State Park and Beach - 10.3 miles
- Abbotts Lagoon Trailhead - 10.9 miles
- Marshall Beach Trailhead - 11.4 miles
- Kehoe Beach Trailhead - 13.0 miles
- Tomales Point Trailhead - 17.0 miles
- McClures Beach Trailhead - 17.1 miles (about 35 minutes)

How to Get to Trailheads South of Bear Valley

All of these trailheads are reached by heading south on Hwy. 1 from the Bear Valley Visitor Center:

- Five Brooks Stables and Trailhead - 4.3 miles
- Randall Trailhead - 6.7 miles (at mile marker 20.53)
- Olema Valley Trailhead - 9.0 miles (at mile marker 18.17)
- Palomarin Trailhead - take the Bolinas turnoff 10 miles from Bear Valley and head south along the the lagoon 1.8 miles to Mesa Road. Turn right and go 4.8 miles (about 30 minutes total).

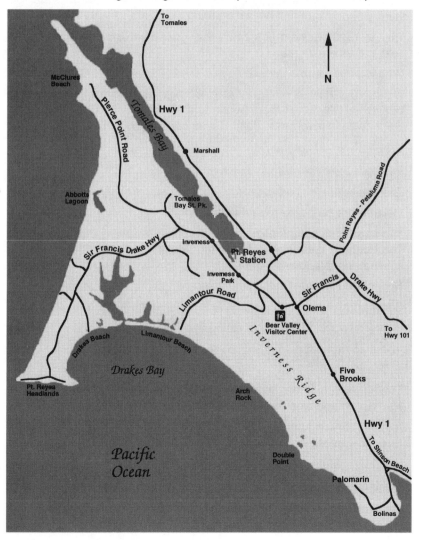

Most Frequently Asked Questions

We asked the rangers at the Bear Valley Visitor Center what questions were asked most often. Here is their list and answers.

RESOURCES

Where is the restroom located?

This is the #1 question asked at the desk. There are two restrooms at Bear Valley. One is located at the entrance to the Visitor Center on the right hand side just before entering the doors.

The second restroom is located 200 yds. east of the Visitor Center next to the picnic area.

Where is the nearest store?

Within three miles of the Visitor Center, there are grocery stores located in Olema, Stinson Beach and Inverness Park. Other stores are located in Inverness, Point Reyes Station and Bolinas.

WHALES

Where is the best place to see whales?

The lighthouse is the best place.

When is the best time to see whales?

The peak of of southern migration is in the first two weeks of January. The northern migration lasts longer, peaking in the middle of March, but extending to the end of May.

How close to shore do the whales come?

Some come within 300 yds., while a half-mile or 800 yds. is common.

How long does it take to get to the lighthouse?

About 45 minutes.

Is it foggy there?

The lighthouse is the second foggiest location on the continent (after Nantucket) and also the windiest point on the West Coast.

It is usually foggy in summer, and less foggy during whale migration. See the Visitor Center bulletin board for current weather information.

HIKING AND WILDFLOWERS

What is the best hike for newcomers to Point Reyes?

Start on the Bear Valley trail. For a 3-mile hike, go out to Divide

Meadow and back. For a good 8-mile hike, go to Arch Rock at the ocean and then retrace your steps back here.

Do you have any maps?

Yes, there is a free trail map available at the desk.

Is there any drinking water on the trails?

Sometimes good drinking water can be found at the backpacking camps. You should carry your own water.

What is the best way to get to Inverness Ridge?

The easiest way is to hike out Bear Valley to Divide Meadow, then take the Old Pine trail up to the ridge.

Where is the best place to see wildflowers?

Chimney Rock, Abbotts Lagoon, Kehoe Beach, the Limantour Beach area and the Coast Trail by Palomarin are generally best.

Are dogs allowed on trails? How about the beach?

Not on trails. Dogs can be taken on a leash on Limantour Beach, Point Reyes Beach North and South, and Kehoe Beach.

OCEAN AND BEACHES

What is the temperature of the ocean?

The average ocean temperature ranges from 50-57 °F.

Is there any place to swim at Point Reyes?

Some people wade at Limantour and Drakes Beach, but there is no lifeguard on duty. Swimming is possible in Tomales Bay, at Marshall Beach and at Tomales Bay State Park. The ocean beaches, Point Reyes Beach, Kehoe and McClures Beach are unsafe for wading.

Are sharks a problem at the beach?

Rarely. However, great white sharks do inhabit the waters.

What is the best beach for families?

The summer is the windiest season at the beach with afternoon northwest winds averaging 15-25 mph. Drakes Beach faces south and provides some shelter. Limantour is good if it is not windy.

RANCHES

Why are there cows in the park?

Legislation creating the park preserved some of the ranches that have been here for over 100 years. The park leases the land to the ranchers, about 21,000 acres or 1/3 of the park area.

Ticks and Lyme Disease

Recent field studies in Marin County show that 1-2% of the western black-legged ticks carry Lyme disease. Since there are several other species of ticks in Marin, this means that the odds of a tick bite producing Lyme disease is much less than 1 in a 100. Even so, Lyme disease can be so severe, it is important to understand the symptoms and prevention techniques.

The Western Black-Legged Tick

The western black-legged tick is the only tick known to carry Lyme disease in California. This tick has three feeding stages in life: larvae, nymph and adult. The larvae and nymph stages are active from late spring to summer and mostly feed on blood from small mammals, lizards and birds.

Adult ticks feed on large mammals and are most commonly found from December through May. The adult female tick is colored red-brown with black legs and is about 1/8" long. The adult male is slightly smaller and entirely brownish-black. They often are found on the tips of grasses and shrubs, along trails and paths, waiting for a host to brush up against them. Ticks do not fly, jump or drop from trees.

Actual Size
Western Black-Legged Tick

How to Avoid Ticks

- Stay on trails. Do not go cross country, especially along deer trails.
- Wear light colored clothing so ticks can be seen. Tuck pant legs into socks.
- Apply an insect repellent, labelled for ticks, to your shoes, socks and pants.
- Check yourself frequently. After passing through tall grass or shrubs, brush your pants or legs.
- After a hike, check yourself completely. Closely check any skin irritation. Ticks anesthetize the skin before biting so you'll seldom feel the original bite.

How to Remove a Tick

Early removal of a tick reduces the risk of infection. Even removal after 36 hours helps. Use tweezers rather than fingers. If you must use fingers, wrap them in a cloth or paper. Lyme disease can be transmitted if tick fluids contact body fluids.

Grab the tick mouth parts as close to the skin as possible and pull straight out. Tick mouth parts have harpoon-like barbs; they do not screw into the skin. If parts break off and remain in the skin, consult a physician.

Wash hands and clean the bite with an antiseptic.

Handle ticks on pets the same way.

Symptoms of Lyme Disease

The first recognizable symptom is usually a ring-like red rash that occurs 3-30 days after the bite of an infected tick. The rash may grow to several inches in diameter, while clearing in the center, thus producing a ring. One or more rashes may occur and not always at the bite site. Unfortunately, a rash only appears in 60-80% of infected persons. Other symptoms may include flu-like fever, chills, fatigue, headaches and a stiff neck.

The second stage of Lyme disease, which may develop weeks to months later, includes meningitis, encephalitis, facial paralysis, abnormal heart beats, numbness and pain in joints, tendons, muscles and bones. These symptoms may last for several weeks or months.

The third stage symptoms occur months to years later and include intermittent arthritis, fatigue, numbness and loss of memory. Lyme disease can also become chronic and produce erosion of cartilage and bone.

Treatment of Lyme Disease

Early diagnosis of Lyme disease is crucial. If you are bitten and later develop these symptoms, see a doctor and get a blood test. Treatment with antibiotics during the first stage can eliminate or decrease the severity of the second and third stage. Antibiotic treatment of the later stages is often, but not always, successful.

It is estimated that there are 10-20 cases of Lyme disease each year in Marin County. The odds of contacting Lyme disease increase as you head north along the coast for two reasons. The western black-legged tick prefers cool, moist areas and the percentage of ticks carrying Lyme disease increases. In Mendocino county, 20% of the western black-legged ticks carry Lyme disease.

1 Bear Valley Interpretive Trails

Distance: Each trail is less than 1 mile
Elevation Change: No more than 100'
Rating: Hiking - 10   All trails in excellent condition.
When to Go: Excellent anytime, best in spring.

These three interpretative trails all have information signs along them explaining the geology, natural history, or Miwok cultures.

Earthquake Trail - 0.6 miles ♿

0.0 This trailhead is located east of the Visitor Center next to the picnic area. The trail is paved the entire way and wheelchair accessible. The trail provides signs and exhibits explaining the great earthquake of 1906.

0.3 Earthquake motion. The Pacific plate jumped 20 feet northward relative to the North American plate.

0.6 Back at the trailhead next to the restroom.

*Acorn Woodpecker
Found on all
three hikes.*

Kule Loklo Trail - 0.7 miles

0.0 This trail starts about 100 yds. north of the Visitor Center and climbs slightly up to a grove of eucalyptus. Notice the woodpecker holes drilled in dead snags.

0.3 Kule Loklo village. This reconstruction of a Coast Miwok village was started in 1976 and continues today. Cultural demonstrations, work parties and festivals are held here every year. Check with the Visitor Center for details.

0.4 Restroom and junction. For a longer way back, you can bear right to pick up the Horse trail as it circles the pasture adding 0.5 miles to the hike. Otherwise, head left and retrace your steps.

0.7 Back at the trailhead north of the Visitor Center.

Morgan - Woodpecker Trails - 0.8 miles

0.0 Start at the main Bear Valley trailhead located at the south end of the parking lot. Take the Morgan trail east as it parallels the road up to the red buildings of the Morgan horse ranch.

0.1 Junction and museum. For an interesting side trip, you can tour the museum that explains the history and workings of the Morgan horse ranch. After that, head left and follow the Woodpecker trail as it skirts the meadow under a canopy of oaks and bays.

0.7 Bear Valley trailhead and Visitor Center.

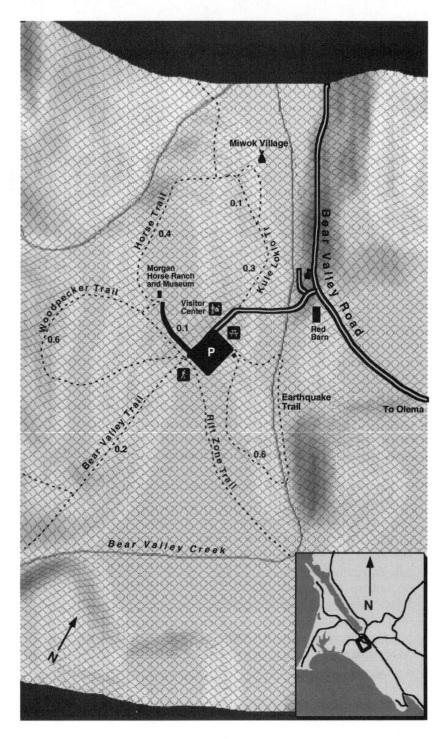

Miwok Village

Horse Trail

0.1

0.4

Kule Lokio Tit

0.3

Morgan
Horse Ranch
and Museum

Visitor
Center

Woodpecker Trail

0.6

0.1

P

Red
Barn

Bear Valley Road

Earthquake
Trail

To Olema

Bear Valley Trail

0.2

Rift Zone Trail

0.6

Bear Valley Creek

N

N

2 Bear Valley - Meadow - Sky Trails

Distance: 4.7 miles
Elevation Change: 1300'
Rating: Hiking - 9   Good trail conditions, but steep in parts.
When to Go: Good anytime, best on clear days in spring.
This hike makes a good round trip to the top of Mt. Wittenberg and back. Great views when clear and good wildflowers in May and June.

0.0 Start at the Bear Valley trailhead south of the parking area.

0.8 Junction #1 with the Meadow trail. Cross the bridge to the right and notice the fallen bay tree straddling the creek. The bay, or California laurel, is very adaptable. It can grow in sun or shade and, when downed, often starts new shoots, as shown here. About 400 yds. farther up the trail, there is another bay with many shoots, this one with twelve large trunks. Although there are occasional bay and tanoak trees here, this is primarily a Douglas fir forest. In winter, after a good rain, look for mushrooms in the forest litter.

1.5 The meadow of the Meadow trail. On the right, you can see the deer-graze line about three feet up on the fir trees. At the north end of the meadow, a fir tree, loaded with cones, provides food for squirrels and seeds for new trees. Douglas fir seeds germinate and survive only when they root in mineral soil and receive direct sunlight. These conditions often occur following a fire. Deer, which are common here, munch new seedlings and help maintain the meadow community.

Mule Deer

The trail reenters the forest and circles a huge bowl-shaped canyon on the left. The understory is lush with huckleberry, sword fern, tanoak and elderberry.

2.3 Two junctions #2. Continue right on the Sky trail towards Mt. Wittenberg. At this point, the trail leaves the forest and enters an open hillside. Up ahead, the trail provides great views of Drakes Bay and the Point Reyes headlands.

2.7 Mt. Wittenberg spur trail. Head uphill for more dramatic views. After exploring the hilltop at 1407', retrace your steps to the Sky trail.

3.1 Junction #3. Take the Sky trail left and start the steep descent towards Bear Valley. Look for views east in the open meadows.

4.7 Bear Valley trailhead. Water and restrooms.

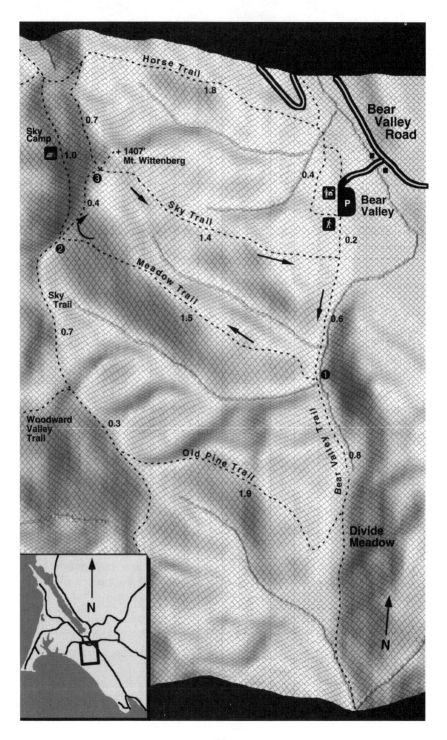

Horse Trail
1.8
0.7
Sky Camp
1.0
+ 1407'
Mt. Wittenberg
❸
0.4
Sky Trail
0.4
Bear Valley Road
Bear Valley
P
0.2
❷
Sky Trail
0.7
Meadow Trail
1.5
1.4
0.6
❶
Woodward Valley Trail
0.3
Old Pine Trail
1.9
0.8
Divide Meadow
N
N

3 Bear Valley - Old Pine - Sky Trails

Distance: 6.9 miles
Elevation Change: 1300'
Rating: Hiking - 10   Good trails, occasionally steep.
When to Go: Excellent anytime, best from March to June.
This is the best and easiest hike to Inverness Ridge. It provides great views, forest vegetation, good berries and spring wildflowers.

0.0 Start at the Bear Valley trailhead at the south end of the parking area and head into the meadow. Most of the grasses are non-native, imported from Mediterranean countries to support livestock.

1.0 About 300 yds. past the junction to the Meadow trail, just before starting uphill, there are two interesting plants growing along the left bank, trillium and wild ginger. Trillium has three symmetrical leaves and in late February and March, produces a beautiful flower with three petals. Ginger has a dark-green, heart-shaped leaf, and from March to June produces deep-purple flowers that are hidden beneath the leaves.

Wild Ginger

1.6 Divide Meadow and junction #1. Take the Old Pine trail right, which provides the easiest climb to the crest of Inverness Ridge. Although called "Old Pine Trail", the trail passes through a magnificent Douglas fir forest.

2.5 Huckleberry lane. Winter rains and summer fog create a luxurious understory, dominated by tall huckleberry shrubs. The best picking is during August and September.

3.5 Junction #2 with the Sky trail. Head right to the north.

3.8 Junction with the Woodward Valley trail. In spring, this verdant meadow, edged with firs offers a peaceful rest stop and picnic area.

4.5 Two junctions #3. The trail leaves the forest here; continue right on the Sky trail towards Mt. Wittenberg. Up ahead, the trail provides great views of Drakes Bay and the Point Reyes headlands.

4.9 Junction #4. Mt. Wittenberg spur trail. If the weather cooperates, head uphill for more dramatic views. Good wildflowers in May.

5.1 Mt. Wittenberg, at 1407'. After exploring the hilltop, retrace your steps to the Sky trail.

5.3 At the junction take the Sky trail left and head downhill.

6.9 Back at the Bear Valley trailhead. Water and restrooms.

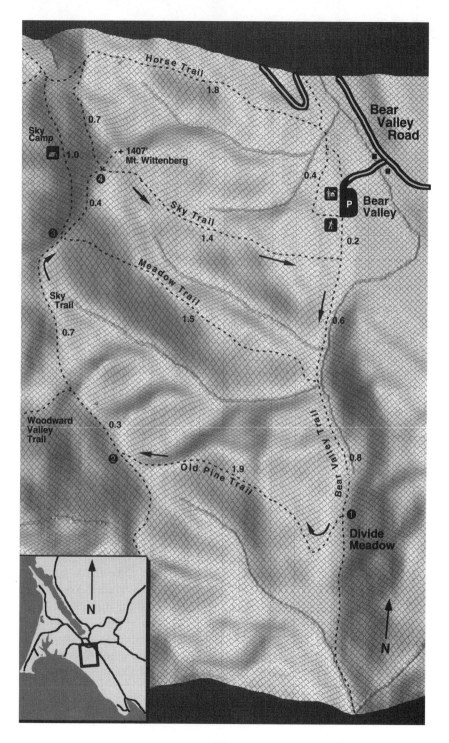

Horse Trail
1.8
0.7
Sky Camp
1.0
+ 1407' Mt. Wittenberg
④
0.4
Sky Trail
1.4
③
Meadow Trail
Sky Trail
0.7
1.5
Woodward Valley Trail
0.3
②
Old Pine Trail 1.9
0.4
Bear Valley Road
P
Bear Valley
0.2
0.6
Bear Valley Trail
0.8
①
Divide Meadow
N
N

4 Bear Valley Trail to Arch Rock

Distance: 8.2 miles
Elevation Change: 400'
Rating: Hiking - 10   Some mud if wet. Bicycles allowed part way.
When to Go: Excellent anytime.
This is the most popular hike on Point Reyes. It is an out and back hike so you can turn around anytime. Great views at Arch Rock.

0.0 Start at the main trailhead south of the parking area.

1.6 Junction #1 at Divide Meadow. In the early 1890s, the Pacific Union Club of San Francisco built a sportsman's lodge here with 35 rooms, stables and kennels. The original plans included a golf course,

tennis courts and swimming pool. Fortunately, the entire resort was never built. The lodge building deteriorated and was removed in 1950. You might be able to discover its location on the far left of the meadow hilltop. Look for amaryllis and other plantings nearby.

3.2 Junction #2 with the Glen and Baldy trails. Bicycles stop here. Continue towards the ocean.

Bear Valley Country Club c. 1895

4.0 Junction with the Coast trail. Head north along the Coast trail for 100 yds. and then take the trail to Arch Rock.

4.1 Arch Rock overlook with great views of the coast. To the south, you can see along Wildcat Beach to Double Point. To the north, you can see Drakes Bay and the Point Reyes headlands.

4.1 Side trip down near the beach. About 50' from the overlook, a short, well-used trail drops steeply down to Coast Creek and out to the beach and ocean. It is worth the trip down to glimpse the sea tunnel (the "arch" of Arch Rock) where the creek meets the ocean.

If conditions are right - low tide, calm ocean and low creek flow - the adventurous hiker can cross the creek and explore the small beach below Arch Rock. Note: Proceed with caution and at your own risk! This is not a park trail. The crossing can be slippery and dangerous. Also be aware of the tide. Do not get yourself trapped on the beach. When you are ready to return, retrace your steps.

8.2 Bear Valley trailhead.

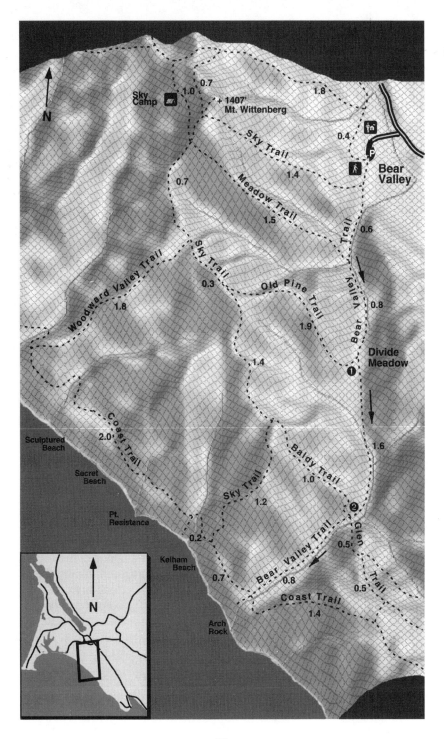

N

Sky Camp

0.7

1.0

+ 1407'
Mt. Wittenberg

1.8

Sky Trail

0.4

1.4

Bear Valley

Meadow Trail

1.5

0.7

0.6

Sky Trail

0.3

Woodward Valley Trail

1.8

Old Pine Trail

1.9

Bear Valley Trail

0.8

Divide Meadow

❶

1.4

Coast Trail

2.0

Sculptured Beach

1.6

Secret Beach

Baldy Trail

1.0

Pt. Resistance

Sky Trail

1.2

❷

0.2

Glen Trail

0.5

Kelham Beach

Bear Valley Trail

0.7

0.8

0.5

Coast Trail

1.4

Arch Rock

N

5 Bear Valley - Sky - Coast Trails

Distance: 10.5 miles
Elevation Change: 1500'
Rating: Hiking - 9   Moderately steep in places.
When to Go: Excellent anytime, best in May.
This hike takes the steepest route to the Inverness Ridge and then follows the ridge to the coast. Great views and magnificent forests.

0.0 Start at the Bear Valley trailhead, south of the parking area.

0.2 Junction #1 with the Sky Trail, which is guarded by a large bay tree. Turn right and set a slow steady pace to climb the moderately steep trail to the ridge. Occasionally, in the open areas, stop and enjoy the views back east across Olema Valley.

1.6 Junction #2. The trail crests Inverness Ridge at 1250' offering spectacular views of Drakes Bay and the headlands with Coast Camp below in the foreground. For a side trip, you can climb to the top of Mt. Wittenberg. Otherwise, head left on the Sky trail.

2.0 Two junctions. Continue south on the Sky trail as it enters a dramatic Douglas fir forest kept refreshingly moist by winter rains and summer fog. The luxuriant understory is filled with ferns, elderberrry, hedge nettle and huckleberry.

2.7 Junction #3 with the Woodward Valley trail. Continue south past this picturesque meadow edged with Douglas fir. Over the next half-mile, look for gooseberry, elderberry, huckleberry and thimbleberry.

Coyote Bush

4.4 Junction #4 with the Baldy trail. Continue straight. This area produces some of the densest stands of coyote bush on Point Reyes. Coyote bush, called "fuzzy wuzzy" because of the white fluff produced on the seeds of the female plant in early summer, dominates the coastal scrub community. Other plants in this "soft chaparral" community include coffeeberry, blackberry, poison oak and sword fern. This is a good place to find brush rabbits, wrentits and the white-crowned sparrow. Up ahead, the trail descends steeply towards the ocean.

5.6 Junction #5. Take the Coast trail left.

6.3 Junction #6. Head right to explore Arch Rock. (See Hike 4 for details.) The hike continues left on the Bear Valley trail.

10.5 Bear Valley trailhead with full facilities.

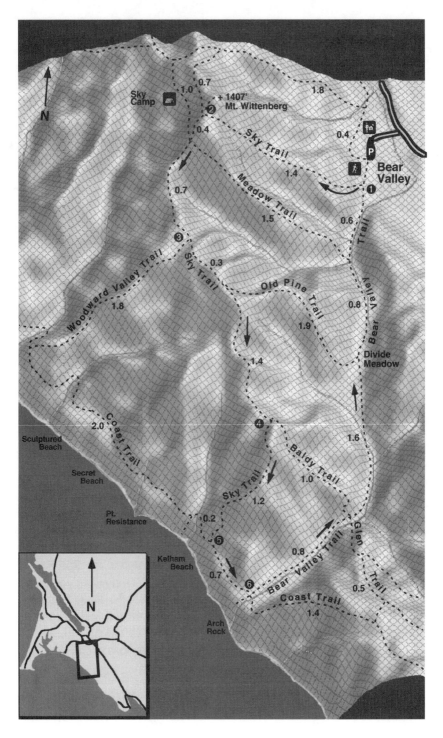

N

1.0   0.7   + 1407'
Sky   Mt. Wittenberg   1.8
Camp   ②

0.4   0.4

Sky Trail   P
                                              Bear
                              1.4   Valley
0.7   ①
            Meadow Trail
                        1.5   0.6

③   Sky Trail   0.3
                          Old Pine Trail

Woodward Valley Trail   0.8

1.8   1.9

                                      Divide
                                      Meadow
            1.4

2.0   Coast Trail   1.6
Sculptured
Beach

Secret   ④
Beach   Baldy Trail
                                   1.0
Pt.   Sky Trail
Resistance   1.2

        0.2
        ⑤   0.8
Kelham   Bear Valley Trail   Glen Trail
Beach
        0.7   ⑥   0.5
                    Coast Trail
                              1.4
            Arch
            Rock

N

20

6 Bear Valley - Glen Camp - Coast Trails

Distance: 11.6 miles
Elevation Change: 950'
Rating: Hiking - 10   Trail is steep along the coast, can be wet.
When to Go: Excellent anytime, best when calm and clear.

This is one of the premier hikes on Point Reyes that includes a riparian corridor, lush forest, breathtaking views and spring flowers.

0.0 Start at the Bear Valley trailhead, south of the parking area.

0.5 Floods and alders. People still talk about the storm of 1982. Bear Valley was completely blocked by flood debris and over one-half of the trail was destroyed. One of the few remaining signs of the flood are groves of young red alders that seeded the following spring. In time, these alders will get much larger, once again shading the trail.

3.2 Junction #1 with Glen trail. Take the Glen trail across the creek and head uphill out of the lush riparian corridor of alder, elderberry, ferns and mosses and into firs, bays, hazelnut, and forget-me-nots.

3.7 Junction #2. Take the Glen Camp Loop trail left. (Note: You can short-cut the hike by 0.7 miles by staying on the Glen trail.)

4.6 Glen Camp with tables and water. This is the prettiest of the backpacking camps, nestled in a small meadow surrounded by oaks and firs. Look for iris under the oaks in spring. Campers will find lots of wildlife, especially at dusk. The trail continues from the west side of the meadow where it begins a moderately steep climb to the ridge.

5.3 Two junctions #3. Take the second right, the signed Coast/Glen spur trail west towards the ocean.

5.5 Junction #4 with Coast trail. Bear right. You may have to wade through one to two inches of water in winter time. The trail heads north across open coastal grasslands. Watch for deer.

6.0 Junction and seasonal pond. Continue left on the Coast trail.

6.3 Outcropping, wildflowers, picnic spot and viewpoint. As you look south along Drakes Bay, the largest prominence is Pt. Resistance. The trail begins a moderate descent. Down below and further west, look for a breathtaking view south towards Double Point.

7.4 Junction with Arch Rock trail. Head left to explore Arch Rock.

7.5 Arch Rock, point #5 . (See Hike 4 for details on getting to the beach.) To return, follow the signs back along the Bear Valley trail.

11.6 Bear Valley trailhead.

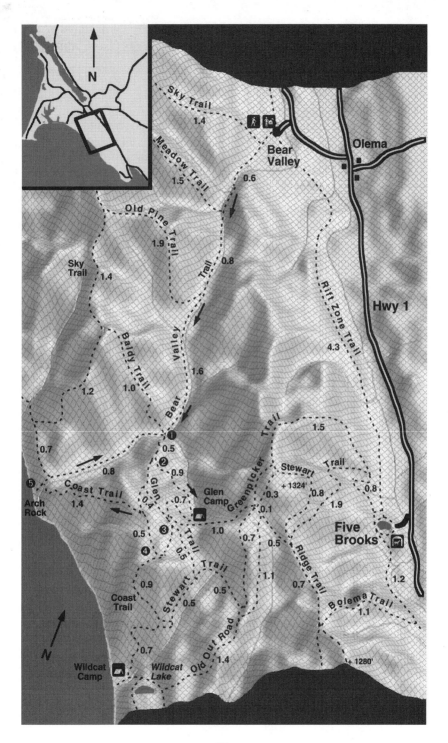

7 Bear Valley - Sky - Woodward - Coast

Distance: 11.6 miles
Elevation Change: 1700'
Rating: Hiking - 10   Good trail conditions. Steep in places.
When to Go: Excellent anytime, best when clear and calm.
This hike has it all! Meadows, forests, creeks, beaches, rolling hills, wildflowers and panoramic views all await the vigorous hiker.

0.0 Start at the Bear Valley trailhead at the south end of the parking area. Look for deer in the meadow, especially in the early morning.

0.2 Junction #1 with the Sky Trail. Head right and start a moderately steep climb under tanoak and Douglas fir.

1.6 Junction #2. The trail crests Inverness Ridge offering dramatic views over Coast Camp to Drakes Bay and the headlands. If the weather is clear, you can take a short side trip and climb 300' to the top of Mt. Wittenberg. Otherwise, head left on the Sky trail.

2.0 Two junctions. Continue south on the Sky trail as it enters a dense Douglas fir forest. In the understory, lush, light-green elderberry presents a striking contrast to the tall, dark fir canopy.

2.7 Junction #3 with Woodward Valley trail. Turn right and head west to follow the trail as it rolls downhill through meadow, forest and open coastal ridges.

3.7 Ocean views. The trail levels off, then climbs to a hilltop 530' above the ocean. This scenic viewpoint offers a panoramic sweep from the Point Reyes headlands to Double Point.

4.5 Junction #4 with Coast trail. Bear left and head south.

6.5 Kelham Beach access trail. In the summer and fall, at tides below plus one foot, the adventurous hiker can walk along Kelham Beach and take the sea tunnel up to Arch Rock. (See Hike 4 for more details). Otherwise, continue south on the Coast trail.

7.4 Junction #5 with Arch Rock trail. Head right.

7.5 Arch Rock. (See Hike 4 for exploring Arch Rock.) To complete the hike, follow the Bear Valley trail inland as it parallels the creek.

7.7 Buckeye trees. Two large, gnarled buckeyes with twisted trunks stand guard along the right of the trail. Buckeyes produce fraqrant flowers in late spring, then soon after, in early summer, begin losing their leaves.

11.6 Bear Valley trailhead. Visitor Center, water and restrooms.

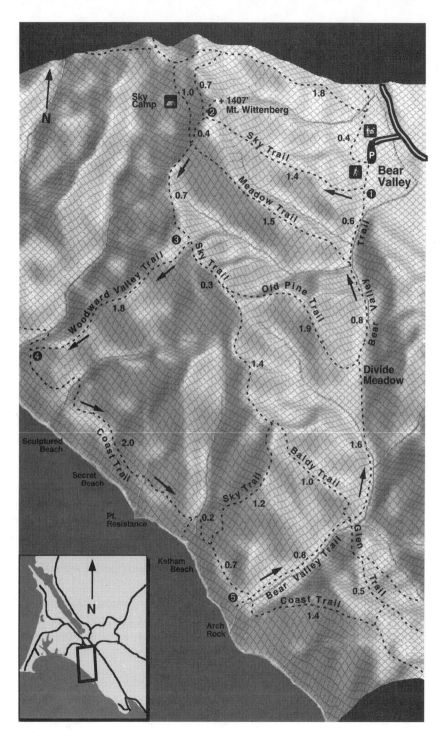

N

Sky Camp

+ 1407'
Mt. Wittenberg

Sky Trail

Meadow Trail

0.7

1.0

0.7

0.4

0.7

1.8

0.4

1.4

0.6

② ③

Woodward Valley Trail

Sky Trail

0.3

1.8

Old Pine Trail

1.9

0.8

Bear Valley Trail

① Bear Valley
P

④

1.4

Divide
Meadow

Sculptured
Beach

Coast Trail

2.0

Secret
Beach

Sky Trail

1.2

Baldy Trail

1.6

1.0

Pt.
Resistance

0.2

Kelham
Beach

0.7

0.8

Bear Valley Trail

Glen Trail

0.5

⑤

Coast Trail

1.4

Arch
Rock

N

8 Olema Valley - Bolema - Stewart

Distance: 6.2 miles
Elevation Change: 1100'
Rating: Hiking - 9   Trail conditions good.
When to Go: Excellent anytime.
This hike makes a loop around the eastern side of Inverness Ridge through a dense Douglas fir forest.

0.0 Start at the Five Brooks trailhead and take the main trail northwest past the artificial pond and towards Inverness Ridge.

0.2 Junction #1. Take the Olema Valley trail left around the pond 100 yds., then bear right at the second junction. The trail heads south through an enchanting forest of Douglas fir, bay and alder with a dense understory of ferns, hazelnut, ginger, nettles and blackberry.

Up ahead, the trail crosses a bridge, then starts a moderately steep climb in more open forest.

1.4 Junction #2. Head right on the Bolema trail and continue to climb. Farther up the trail, you'll see the first stand of Monterey pines that were seeded after logging operations in the late 1950s.

2.5 Junction #3 at the highest point of the hike at 1180'. Head right on the Ridge trail. Occasionally, you get glimpses west to the ocean.

3.1 Forest and berries. The trail enters a dark Douglas fir forest with lots of huckleberries that ripen from July through September. The forest is often damp in the summertime due to heavy fog drip.

3.2 Junction #4. The Ridge trail goes left. Continue straight here and right at the next junction 100 yds. ahead.

3.3 Junction. Take the Stewart trail downhill to the right. The old roadbed was once paved and wide enough for two lanes of traffic. Watch for an occasional large, old-growth Douglas fir on the edge of the roadbed. These trees were left by loggers to support the road and to provide seeds for future trees.

5.2 Junction #5 with the Greenpicker trail. Continue downhill. Up ahead, the trail makes a large hairpin turn in a steep canyon and creek. Look for five-finger ferns along the bank. In June, an aralia with large 12" leaves, and even larger flower stalks, blooms along the moist banks.

6.0 Junction and mill pond. Head left.

6.2 Trailhead with picnic tables, water and restrooms.

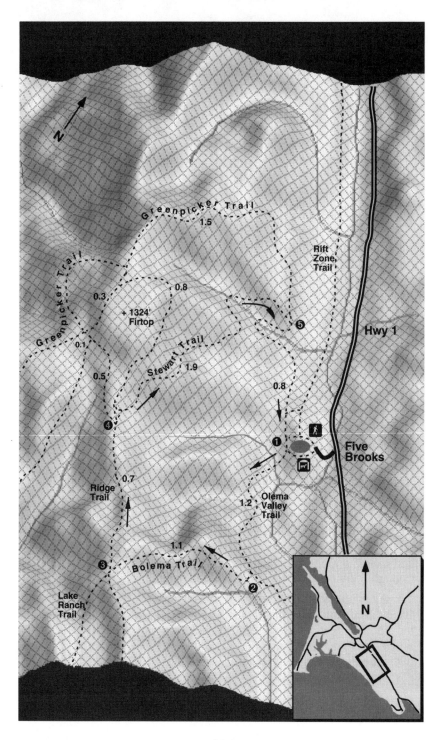

N

Greenpicker Trail
1.5

Greenpicker Trail

Rift
Zone
Trail

0.3   0.8

+ 1324'
Firtop

Hwy 1

0.1

Stewart Trail

0.5   1.9

❺

4

0.8

❶   Five
Brooks

Olema
Valley
Trail

Ridge   0.7
Trail
                 1.2

❸   Bolema Trail

1.1

❷

Lake
Ranch
Trail

N

9 Stewart - Greenpicker Trails

Distance: 6.9 miles
Elevation Change: 1300'
Rating: Hiking - 8   Trail is moderately steep in places.
When to Go: Good anytime, best in February and March.

This hike stays entirely in a scenic Douglas fir forest as it climbs the eastern slopes of Inverness Ridge.

0.0 Start at the Five Brooks parking area and head northwest through the gate. Circle the pond surrounded by willows and alders.

0.2 Junction #1 with the Olema Valley and Stewart trails. Head right and follow the signs to Firtop. The Stewart trail is really a wide road that makes a moderate climb through a Douglas fir forest with occasional bay, alder and tanoak. Ferns and elderberry dominate the understory.

Five-finger Fern

0.7 Hairpin turn. Just past the turn, look for four different ferns on the steep bank - lady fern, sword fern, five-finger fern and chain fern.

1.0 Junction with the Greenpicker trail. Continue left towards Firtop. Up ahead, you'll find stumps of Douglas fir, remnants of the logging operations that ended in the early 1960s.

2.9 Junction #2 with the Ridge trail. Continue on the Stewart trail.

3.7 Junction and Firtop at 1324'. The small meadow at Firtop is surrounded by firs, blocking what were once magnificent views. You can cut the hike short by returning on the Greenpicker trail. Otherwise, continue across the meadow and head downhill.

4.0 Two junctions #3. Go right about 100' on the Ridge trail and pick up the Greenpicker trail to head back towards Five Brooks. The trail first makes a moderate descent for 0.2 miles, then climbs steeply through a very dense forest back up to Firtop.

4.4 Junction #4 with the spur trail to Stewart trail. Continue left on the Greenpicker trail. This part of the hike borders the private property of the Vedanta Society. Up ahead, the terrain becomes more difficult and leaves the road to enter an old growth forest with lots of huckleberries and sword ferns.

5.9 Junction. Head left, downhill on the Stewart trail.

6.9 Five Brooks trailhead with water and restrooms.

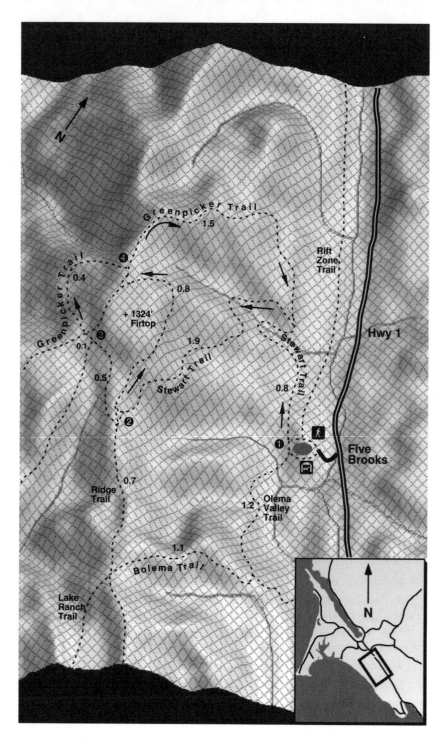

Greenpicker Trail

1.5

Rift Zone, Trail

❹

Greenpicker Trail

0.4

0.8

Greenpicker Trail

+ 1324' Firtop

❸

0.1

Stewart Trail

1.9

0.5

Stewart Trail

0.8

❷

❶

Hwy 1

Five Brooks

0.7

Ridge Trail

1.2

Olema Valley Trail

1.1

Bolema Trail

Lake Ranch Trail

N

N

10 Greenpicker - Coast - Stewart Trails

Distance: 10.3 miles
Elevation Change: 1600'
Rating: Hiking - 8   At times, poison oak crowds the Coast trail.
When to Go: Good anytime, best when clear.
This is a rugged hike that makes a moderately steep climb through dense forest, then provides dramatic views along the coast.

0.0 Start at the Five Brooks parking area and circle the pond bordered by willows and alders. Look for ducks and turtles.

0.2 Junction #1. Head right on the Stewart trail.

1.0 Junction #2. Take the Greenpicker trail right as it heads uphill, then skirts the private Vedanta property. The trail climbs through rugged terrain that supports a luxuriant Douglas fir forest. The tall canopy allows light for a dense growth of ferns and huckleberry.

2.5 Junction with the Stewart trail and Firtop at 1324'. A spur trail leads left to the meadow at Firtop. Continue on the Greenpicker trail.

2.8 Junction #3 with Ridge and Stewart trails. Continue on the Greenpicker trail as it goes right downhill.

3.8 Junction #4 with Glen trail. Go left up the road.

3.9 Two junctions #5. Take the second right, the Coast Spur trail.

4.1 Junction #6 with Coast trail. Head left. Watch out for poison oak.

4.4 Wildcat Camp overlook. Here is one of the premier viewing spots on Point Reyes. The wild-looking, jumbled hills from Wildcat Camp to Bass Lake are mostly the result of massive landslides. See if you can spot evidence of old scarps, large cuts or slides on the western slopes of Inverness Ridge.

5.0 Junction #7 with the Stewart trail. At this point, you can take a side trip to Wildcat Camp and the beach. Otherwise, bear left.

5.5 Junction with Glen trail. Stay right on the Stewart trail.

5.8 Two uncommon shrubs. Just 20' past an exposed cliff, look for a white ceanothus, which flowers in May and below it, a silk tassel shrub, with hanging catkins. Both plants are seldom seen on Point Reyes. Continue on the Stewart trail.

6.7 Junction #8. Take the Ridge trail right to circle Firtop.

7.3 Junction #9. Head left 200' to pick up the Stewart trail.

10.3 Five Brooks trailhead with water and restrooms.

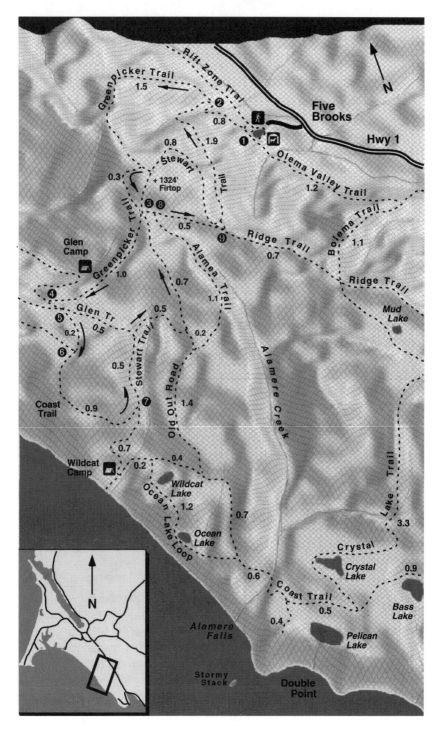

Rift Zone Trail

Greenpicker Trail
1.5

❷
0.8

Five
Brooks

Hwy 1

🚶 ❶ 🏠

0.8   1.9

0.8

Stewart

Olema Valley Trail
1.2

0.3

+ 1324'
Firtop

❸ ❽

0.5

Ridge   Trail

0.7

Bolema Trail
1.1

Trail

❾

Ridge   Trail

Glen
Camp

Greenpicker Trail

1.0

Alamea Trail

0.7

Mud
Lake

❹

Glen Tr   0.5

0.5

1.1

❺

0.2

0.2

Alamere Creek

❻

0.5

Stewart Trail

Coast
Trail

0.9

❼

Old   Out Road

1.4

0.7

0.4

Lake   Trail

Wildcat
Camp

0.2

Wildcat
Lake

Ocean Lake Loop

1.2

0.7

3.3

Ocean
Lake

Crystal

Crystal
Lake

0.9

0.6

Coast   Trail

0.5

Bass
Lake

Alamere
Falls

0.4

Pelican
Lake

Stormy
Stack

Double
Point

N

30

11 Randall - Olema Valley - Bolema

Distance: 9.8 miles
Elevation Change: 1200'
Rating: Hiking - 7   Trails may be muddy or overgrown in parts.
When to Go: Best in April and May after the ground dries a bit.
This loop hike follows the earthquake topography of Olema Valley,
then climbs the heavily forested Inverness Ridge.

0.0 Start at the Randall trailhead located near mile marker 20.53 on
Highway 1. Take the Randall Spur trail west along a bank of willows
heading towards Inverness Ridge. Look for warblers in the willows.

0.4 Junction #1. Head right on the Olema Valley trail and start a
gentle climb through a mixture of open grassland and oak, bay, and fir
trees. The trail can be muddy or dusty depending on the season.

Occasionally, look back to view the jumbled topography of the San
Andreas rift zone. It is estimated that the Inverness Ridge to the west
is moving 1.3" per year relative to the Bolinas Ridge to the east. This
motion adds up to more than 1000' over the last 10,000 years.

1.7 Junction #2 with the Bolema trail. Head left to climb the old ranch
road towards the ridge. This is mostly Douglas fir forest with ferns,
hazelnut, hedge nettle, cow parsnip and thimbleberries in the
understory. Look for stands of non-native Monterey pine up ahead.

2.4 Narrow view. As the trail doglegs left, a narrow view opens up
through the trees to the north. On a clear day, you can just see the
jutting profile of Mt. Saint Helena over 40 miles to the northeast.

2.8 Junction #3. Take the Ridge trail left and head south on the ridge.

3.1 Tree stumps and succession. Clearcut logging along the ridge in
the late 1950s opened the way for manzanita to establish itself. Now,
the second generation firs have formed a dense canopy shading out
the manzanita and causing dieback.

5.3 Junction #4. Take the Teixeira trail left. Watch for stinging nettles.

6.0 Junction with the Pablo Point trail. Continue downhill on the
Teixeira trail. Ahead, trail conditions deteriorate as horses and water
have created deep ruts with exposed roots and jagged rocks.

7.1 Junction #5. The trail crosses a bog right before the junction.
Head left on the Olema Valley trail through an open meadow.

9.4 Junction. Take the Randall Spur trail east.

9.8 Back at the trailhead. If grass crowded the trail, check for ticks.

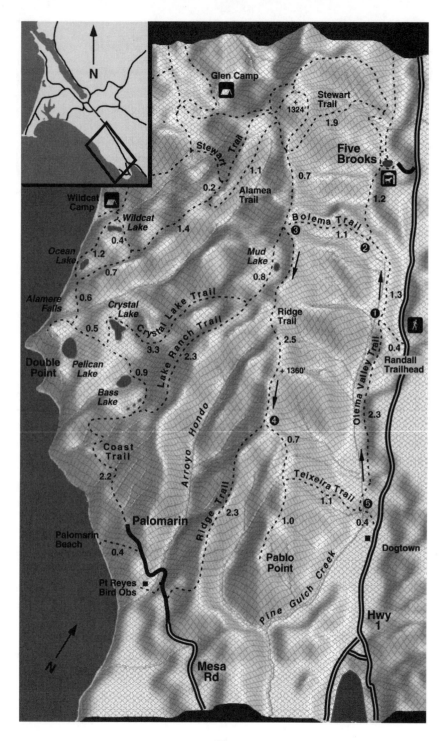

Glen Camp

Stewart Trail
+ 1324'

Stewart Trail
1.9

Stewart Trail

1.1

0.2

Alamea Trail

0.7

Five Brooks

1.2

Wildcat Camp

Wildcat Lake

1.4

Bolema Trail

❸

1.1

❷

0.4

Ocean Lake

1.2

0.7

Mud Lake

0.8

1.3

Alamere Falls

0.6

Crystal Lake Trail

❶

0.5

Crystal Lake

Ridge Trail

0.4

Randall Trailhead

3.3

Lake Ranch Trail

2.3

2.5

Double Point

Pelican Lake

0.9

+ 1360'

Bass Lake

2.3

Otema Valley Trail

Coast Trail

❹

0.7

2.2

Arroyo Hondo

Teixeira Trail

1.1

❺

0.4

Palomarin

Ridge Trail

2.3

1.0

Dogtown

Palomarin Beach

0.4

Pablo Point

Pt Reyes Bird Obs

Pine Gulch Creek

Hwy 1

Mesa Rd

N

12 PRBO Nature and Beach Trails

Distance: Two separate hikes of 0.5 and 0.8 miles
Elevation Change: 250' for the Palomarin Beach trail.
Rating: Hiking - 10
When to Go: Excellent anytime, beach trail best at low tide.

The Point Reyes Bird Observatory Nature trail explores a magnificent small canyon with dense growth. The beach trail leads to tidepools.

Point Reyes Bird Observatory Nature Trail - 0.5 miles

0.0 (Note: An interpretative pamphlet is available at the PRBO Visitor Center.) Start at the PRBO parking lot and take the nature trail south past coyote bush and wind-pruned fir trees. At 100 yds., notice the tough, scrub oak trees growing close to the ground.

Up ahead, the trail heads steeply down into Fern Canyon guarded by twisted buckeye trees covered with old man's beard - a grey-green lichen hanging in the branches. This little canyon provides a rain forest habitat of robust flora and noisy birds. Look for several kinds of ferns and berries - sword fern, five-finger fern, chain fern, blackberries and thimbleberries - under a canopy of buckeye trees.

0.1 The trail crosses the creek and climbs out the other side. A multi-trunked buckeye stands over patches of Solomon's seal.

Continue across the bluff to a 4-way junction marked by three posts on your left. If the trail is not overgrown with blackberries and thimbleberries, head left through the posts to the road. Otherwise retrace your steps.

0.2 Road. Go left past the exposed shale cliffs.

0.5 Entrance to PRBO.

Palomarin Beach Trail - 0.8 miles

0.0 Start at the trailhead 0.3 miles north of the Point Reyes Bird Observatory. Follow the trail as it heads down past eucalyptus, sage and coastal scrub towards the beach. Look for wildflowers in spring.

Up ahead, a sign cautions visitors to watch for slippery rocks and large waves. This spot also offers great views south down the coast and northwest across Drakes Bay to the Point Reyes headlands.

0.3 Hollow. The trail skirts the edge of a wet hollow, then drops down to the beach.

0.4 Beach. You can explore in both directions from here.

0.8 Parking area.

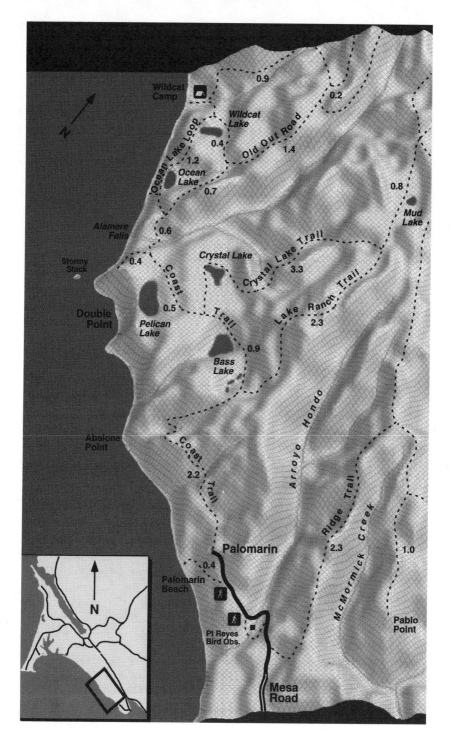

13 Coast Trail to Double Point

Distance: 8.0 miles
Elevation Change: 550'
Rating: Hiking - 9   The trail passes very close to steep cliffs.
When to Go: Excellent anytime, best from December to July.
Double Point provides one of the best view spots on the west coast.
In season, look for whales, seals and wildflowers.

0.0 Start at 260' at the Palomarin parking area. Take the dirt road up towards the eucalyptus grove. In spring, look for lupine, cow parsnip, Indian paintbrush, iris, wild cucumber and poppies.

2.0 Small pass. After heading inland into a large ravine, the trail makes a long climb up through a narrow rocky pass at 580'. These outcroppings of chert, shale and sandstone are marine deposits, part of a sedimentary layer that covers most of the southern seashore.

2.2 Junction #1 with the Lake Ranch Trail. Continue left.

2.7 Bass Lake. The first glimpse through the willows and coyote bush provides an enticing view of this lovely lake.

2.8 Unmarked junction. A spur trail left explores the lake shoreline. On warm days, you'll often find picnickers and swimmers here. The hike continues uphill into a small fir forest where ferns, ceanothus and coffeeberry offer a nice change of pace from the open hillsides.

3.3 Pelican Lake. Across the lake, a small notch between Double Point allows overflow in wet years. Pelican Lake and the lakes in this area were formed by landslides that blocked normal drainage.

3.6 Two junctions #2 (see map - inset). At the first junction at the north end of the lake, take the spur trail left. Note: At the second junction 150' beyond, another spur trail goes left 0.5 miles to the top of Alamere Falls. This trail is unmaintained, dangerous and overgrown with poison oak.

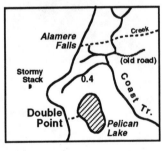

4.0 Double Point at 490'. This spot provides commanding views of the coastline and hills inland. (Stay well back from the cliffs edge!) In winter and spring, look for whales in the ocean. Also check the beaches below for harbor seals that breed here from May to July. When done, retrace your steps.

8.0 Palomarin trailhead. Restrooms, but no water.

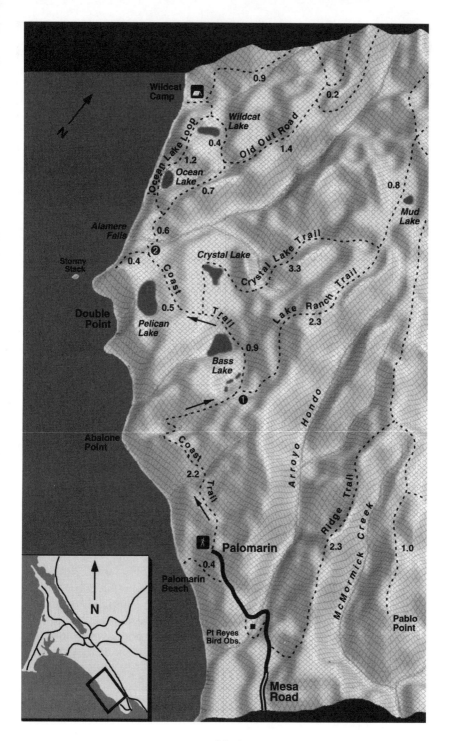

Wildcat Camp

Wildcat Lake

0.9

0.2

Ocean Lake Loop

0.4

Old Out Road

1.4

Ocean Lake

1.2

0.7

0.8

Mud Lake

Alamere Falls

0.6

Crystal Lake Trail

Stormy Stack

0.4

②

Coast

Crystal Lake

3.3

Lake Ranch Trail

Double Point

0.5

Trail

2.3

Pelican Lake

0.9

Bass Lake

①

Abalone Point

Arroyo Hondo

Coast

2.2

Trail

Ridge Trail

Palomarin

2.3

1.0

McMormick Creek

0.4

Palomarin Beach

Pablo Point

Pt Reyes Bird Obs.

Mesa Road

N

N

14 Ridge - Lake Ranch - Coast Trails

Distance: 11.2 miles
Elevation Change: 1200'
Rating: Hiking - 9   May be overgrown. Some poison oak and mud.
When to Go: Excellent anytime, best in spring when clear.

This hike climbs the southern end of Inverness Ridge north into a magnificent fir forest, then drops through a massive landslide area.

0.0 Park in the Point Reyes Bird Observatory parking lot. Take the signed Nature trail down into a small canyon featuring luxuriant growth and striking buckeye trees. Cross the creek and immediately head up the other side. Follow the trail across the plateau to a four-way junction marked by three short poles on your left. Head left past the poles and through dense blackberry vines towards the road.

0.2 Main road. Head right down the dirt road.

0.4 Junction #1 with the Ridge trail. Turn left and start a moderately steep climb through coastal scrub dotted with wind-pruned Douglas fir. The trail may be overgrown in places.

1.6 Views. Good views east to Pablo Point and beyond to Bolinas Ridge and south to Bolinas Lagoon.

Up ahead, the trail enters a dense conifer forest that covers the Inverness Ridge from here to Point Reyes Hill ten miles north.

2.7 Junction #2 with the Teixeira trail. Continue north on the ridge.

3.6 Mountain top at 1340'. A large moss-covered Douglas fir stands at the highest point on the southern ridge. This area was heavily logged in the late '50s which allowed manzanita to spread. Now the manzanita is dying out under the shade of the second growth of fir.

5.2 Junction #3. Take the Lake Ranch trail to the left. Up ahead, Mud Lake provides a home to red-winged blackbirds.

6.0 Junction with Crystal Lake trail. Continue on the Lake Ranch trail.

7.1 Views and landslides. The trail heads south and the vegetation opens up providing great views of the coast below and the headlands north. On your left, look for evidence of the massive slides that reshaped the landscape and created a series of ponds and lakes below. For the next mile, try to imagine how these slides took place.

8.3 Junction #4. Head left on the Coast trail.

10.5 Palomarin trailhead #5. Continue on the road south.

11.2 PRBO parking area. No facilities.

37

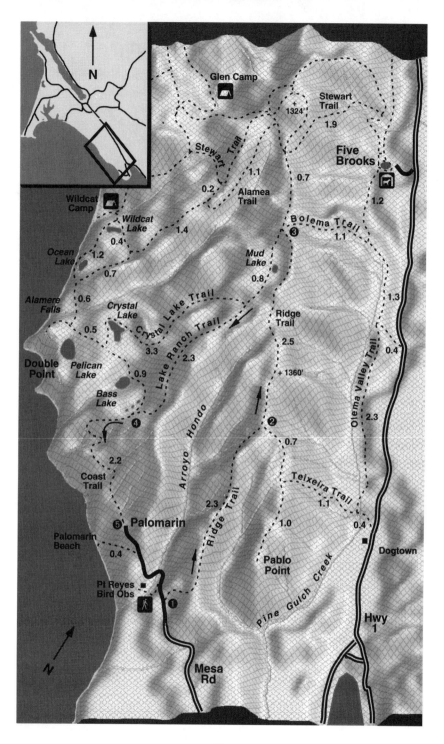

15 Coast Trail to Wildcat Camp

Distance: 11.6 miles
Elevation Change: 1000'
Rating: Hiking - 9
When to Go: Good anytime, best in April and May.

This hike takes the Coast trail past ponds and lakes to Wildcat Camp where you can make a side trip to Alamere Falls. Good views.

0.0 Start at 260' at the Palomarin parking area. Take the dirt road up towards the eucalyptus grove. A National Park interpretative sign and primitive restroom are located at opposite ends of the grove.

0.6 Coastal views. The trail skirts the cliff offering dramatic views both north and south. In spring, the green hills are dotted with blue lupine, white cow parsnip and the red or yellow Indian paintbrush. Other spring wildflowers include iris, wild cucumber and poppy.

2.2 Junction #1 with Lake Ranch trail. Continue left. Up ahead, the trail passes several small ponds formed by slumping soil. All of the ponds and lakes in this area were formed thousands of years ago by massive landslides that blocked normal creek drainage.

2.7 Bass Lake. Coastal scrub edges the southern shore of Point Reyes' most picturesque lake while Douglas fir frames the north side.

2.8 Unmarked junction. A spur trail left explores Bass Lake.

3.6 Three junctions, see map inset for Hike 13. Continue on Coast trail.

4.2 Junction #2 with Ocean Lake Loop. Head left. Pause for views.

Bass Lake

4.4 Unmarked junction with an unmaintained spur trail to Wildcat Beach. Continue north towards Ocean Lake and Wildcat Lake.

5.4 Junction #3 with the Coast trail. Head left.

6.1 Wildcat Camp. Water and restrooms available. For a side trip, walk south along the beach 1.1 miles to the 40' Alamere Falls. Alamere Creek flows all year, but is most spectacular in the spring and after heavy rains. For the return trip, take the Coast trail south towards Palomarin.

11.6 Palomarin trailhead. Restrooms, but no water.

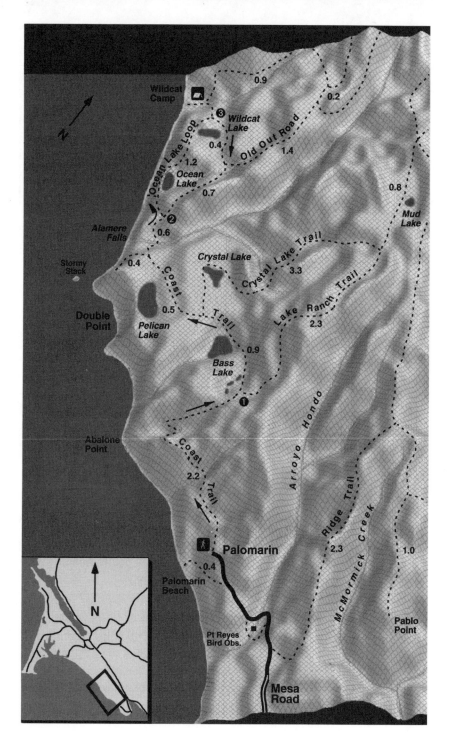

Wildcat
Camp

0.9

0.2

❸ Wildcat
Lake

Ocean Lake Loop

0.4

Old Out Road

1.4

0.8

Mud
Lake

1.2

Ocean
Lake

0.7

Alamere
Falls

❷

0.6

Crystal Lake

Crystal Lake Trail

3.3

Lake Ranch Trail

Stormy
Stack

0.4

Coast

Double
Point

0.5

Pelican
Lake

Trail

2.3

0.9

Bass
Lake

❶

Arroyo Hondo

Abalone
Point

Coast

2.2

Trail

Ridge Trail

Palomarin

2.3

1.0

McMormick Creek

0.4

Palomarin
Beach

Pt Reyes
Bird Obs.

Pablo
Point

Mesa
Road

N

16 Sky - Horse - Mt. Wittenberg Trails

Distance: 4.5 miles
Elevation Change: 750'
Rating: Hiking - 10   Trail conditions good.
When to Go: Excellent anytime, best in late spring.
This is the easiest hike to the top of Mt. Wittenberg. When clear, the hike provides great views in all directions. Good wildflowers in May.

0.0 Start at the Sky trailhead about 3.5 miles out the Limantour Road. The trail is an old ranch road that climbs south through a Douglas fir forest lush with berries, nettles and ferns.

0.7 Junction #1. Take the Horse trail left. At the start of the trail, notice the large patch of salal with bright green, shiny leaves . Up ahead, the trail circles a steep canyon bare of conifers. The canyon's bowl shape suggests that a large slide occurred. In winter, water from a spring seeps out of the hillside, and may cause further soil erosion.

1.1 Junction #2. The vegetation opens up to provide good views north. The large flat mountain due north is Point Reyes Hill at 1336'. Turn right and head uphill on the Mt. Wittenberg trail.

1.2 More evidence of slides. The trail doubles back above the large canyon. Here is where the slide must have started. Notice the large firs above the trail. Also, notice there is much less seepage. Up ahead, the view north gets better. You can just get a glimpse of Mt. Saint Helena 40 miles northeast in Sonoma County.

1.8 Junction #3 and more views. Drakes Bay and the Point Reyes headlands provide a nice background to the grassy slopes of Mt. Wittenberg and Sky Camp below. Take the Mt. Wittenberg trail up to the top. Look for tidy tips and lupine in May and June.

2.0 Mt. Wittenberg at 1407'. This is the highest point on Point Reyes. Circle the broad mountain top and enjoy the views before heading back down. Look for deer along the southern hilltops.

2.2 Junction. Take the Sky trail southwest, down along the ridge line.

2.8 Two junctions #4. Take the Sky trail right towards Sky Camp.

3.3 Sky Camp and spring. To explore the spring take the short spur trail to the left. When done, continue down the road past the restroom.

3.8 Junction and rock exposure. Just before the junction, slabs of sedimentary rock, called Monterey shale, lie exposed along the trail.

4.5 Back at the trailhead. No facilities.

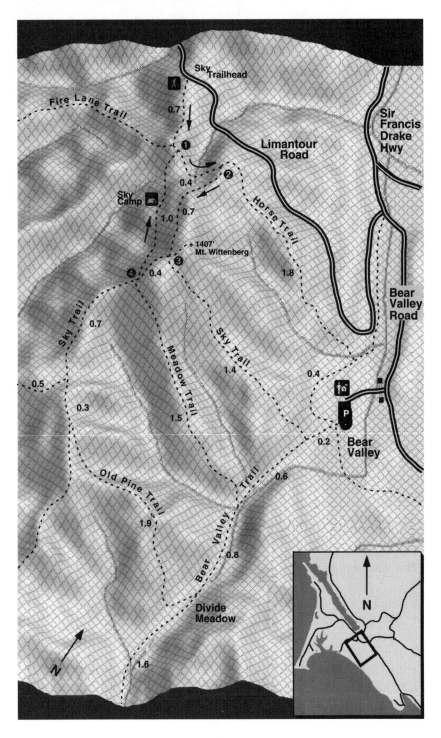

Sky Trailhead

Limantour Road

Sir Francis Drake Hwy

Fire Lane Trail

0.7

①

0.4

②

Sky Camp

0.7

1.0

Horse Trail

1.8

Bear Valley Road

+ 1407'
Mt. Wittenberg

③

④ 0.4

Sky Trail

0.7

0.4

0.5

Meadow Trail

0.3

Sky Trail

1.4

1.5

P

0.2

Bear Valley

0.6

Old Pine Trail

1.9

Bear Valley Trail

0.8

N

Divide Meadow

N

1.6

17 Sky - Fire Lane - Laguna Trails

Distance: 6.2 miles
Elevation Change: 850'
Rating: Hiking - 9   Moderately steep in places, can be wet.
When to Go: Good anytime. Try early morning in winter for views.

This trail provides interesting terrain as it rolls down a ridgeline from Mt. Wittenberg. Early morning sunshine makes the headlands glow.

0.0 Start at the Sky trailhead about 3.5 miles along the Limantour Road. About 200 yds. up the trail, where it breaks into the open, look for Bishop pine to the right of the trail. This is a good hike for comparing Douglas fir and Bishop pine. Douglas fir have small, one-inch needles sprayed around a stem. Bishop Pine have two needles per bunch, each three inches long. The cones of the Bishop pine are bigger, harder and heavier.

Most of this hike takes place in a transition zone between Douglas fir and Bishop pine communities.

Bishop Pine   Douglas Fir

0.7 Junction #1 with Fire Lane trail. Take a right and follow the trail as it skirts the hilltop. The trail climbs slightly to 1090' then starts a moderate descent towards the ocean.

1.0 Great views. The trail descends through a mixture of forest and open coastal scrub opening up great views of the rolling hills, Drakes Bay and the Farallon Islands.

2.0 The trail is deceptive. You expect it to be all downhill, but it climbs several knolls, each one bringing different views.

2.9 Junction #2. Often, you can hear frogs from a marsh 300 yds. to the south. The Laguna trail heads north here. After heavy rains, there may be standing water up ahead. In some places, the trail consists of fine, granular soil. When wet, look for animal tracks.

3.7 Junction #3 with the road and the ranger residence at 140'. Stay on the Laguna trail as it heads uphill to the right. Notice the large, old buckeye trees with their multiple trunks covered with moss and lichen. Up ahead, look for trillium and Solomon's seal in early spring.

4.0 Junction with the Hidden Valley trail. Continue straight. At the end of the grassy meadow, the trail starts a moderate climb northeast.

5.5 Junction #4 with the Bayview trail. Turn right and head southeast.

6.2 Sky trailhead. No facilities.

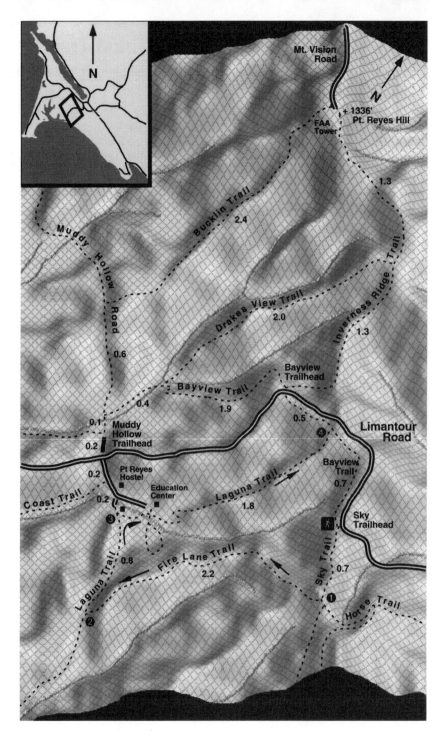

Mt. Vision
Road

N

+ 1336'
Pt. Reyes Hill

FAA
Tower

1.3

Bucklin Trail
2.4

Muddy Hollow Road

Drakes View Trail
2.0

Inverness Ridge Trail
1.3

0.6

Bayview
Trailhead

Bayview Trail
0.4   1.9

0.5

Limantour
Road

0.1

Muddy
Hollow
Trailhead

0.2

❹

Bayview
Trail
0.7

0.2

Pt Reyes
Hostel

Laguna Trail

Coast Trail

0.2

Education
Center

1.8

Sky
Trailhead

❸

Laguna Trail

0.8

Fire Lane Trail
2.2

Sky Trail

0.7

❷

❶

Horse Trail

18 Sky-Woodward Valley-Coast Trails

Distance: 9.4 miles
Elevation Change: 1100'
Rating: Hiking - 9   Sky and Laguna trails can be wet.
When to Go: Excellent anytime, best when clear and calm.
This hike explores the slopes of Mt. Wittenberg down to the ocean. It offers a variety of terrain and views, and beach access.

0.0 Start at the Sky trailhead located 3.5 miles out the Limantour Road and take the the trail south as it climbs towards Sky Camp.

0.7 Two junctions #1. Continue uphill past the Fire Lane trail and the Horse trail which lie about 100 yds. apart.

1.2 Sky Camp. Near the restroom, you can climb a small knoll to the right to get good views of Drakes Bay. The trail continues left.

1.7 Two junctions #2. Bear right and head south past the Meadow trail. The Sky trail rolls downhill along the Inverness Ridge and enters a magnificent Douglas fir forest. Huckleberry, elderberry, ferns and nettles make up the lush understory.

2.4 Junction #3 and meadow. Take the Woodward Valley trail as it heads down through the oval-shaped meadow.

3.9 View point. The trail levels off, then climbs 50' to a hilltop offering commanding views of the coastline. To the south, you can see all the way to Double Point and just below it, Alamere Falls. To the north, you see the sweeping arc of Drakes Bay culminating in the Point Reyes headlands and Chimney Rock.

4.2 Junction #4. Take the Coast trail north. Up ahead, the trail turns inland to cross Santa Maria Creek, then returns to the coast. Look for a large, granite outcropping high above the trail.

5.4 Coast Camp. Water, restrooms and beach access. For a short side trip, explore the beach to the north.

5.5 Junction #5. Take the Fire Lane trail to the right and start a moderate climb through open grassland. Up ahead, the trail passes a marshy area where you may hear frogs croaking.

6.5 Junction #6 with the Laguna trail. Continue right on the Fire Lane trail which climbs more steeply. Watch for two kinds of conifers, the short-needle Douglas fir and the longer-needle Bishop Pine.

8.7 Junction. Head left on the Sky trail.

9.4 Back at the Sky trailhead. No facilities.

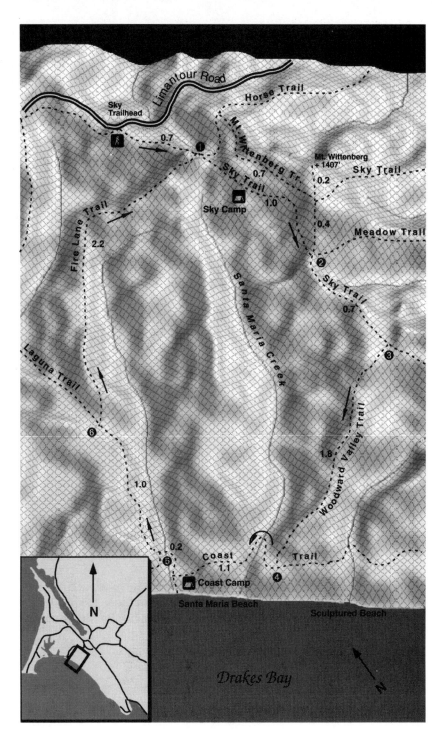

Limantour Road

Sky Trailhead

Horse Trail

Mt. Wittenberg Tr.

0.7

Mt. Wittenberg
+ 1407'

Sky Trail

0.7

0.2

Sky Trail

Sky Camp

1.0

0.4

Meadow Trail

Fire Lane Trail

2.2

Santa Maria Creek

Sky Trail

0.7

Laguna Trail

Woodward Valley Trail

1.8

6

1.0

0.2

Coast

1.1

Trail

5

Coast Camp

4

Santa Maria Beach

Sculptured Beach

N

Drakes Bay

N

19 Bayview - Muddy Hollow - Laguna

Distance: 5.3 miles
Elevation Change: 600'
Rating: Hiking - 9   Trail can be wet in winter.
When to Go: Excellent anytime, best in April and May.

This hike descends the slope of Inverness Ridge offering great views to the west, then enters a lush riparian corridor.

0.0   Start at the Bayview trailhead about 4.7 miles along the Limantour Road. There is parking here for about a dozen cars in an open area adjacent to an old rock quarry. Take Bayview trail west.

The hike starts in a mixture of Bishop pine forest and coastal scrub. The latter includes huckleberry, coffeeberry, coyote bush, ferns, monkeyflower, salal and blackberry.

1.5   The trail drops down into a scenic canyon and riparian corridor dominated by red alder. Nettles, miner's lettuce, sedges and cow parsnip provide a lush, green understory.

The succulent leaves and stems of miner's lettuce, also known as Indian lettuce, provided a nourishing treat for earlier inhabitants.

1.9   Junction with Drakes View trail. Continue left. Up ahead, the trail crosses a wooden bridge, then passes through a small marshy area. Farther ahead, majestic old buckeyes, their *Miner's Lettuce* contorted branches covered with lichen, overhang the trail.

2.3   Junction #1 with the Muddy Hollow road. Head left and watch for birds along the creek and in the marsh.

2.6   Junction #2 with the Limantour Road. Cross the road and continue along the pavement past the hostel. Follow the signs to the Laguna trailhead.

3.0   Junction #3 with the Laguna trail. Just past the residence, take the Laguna trail left. Up ahead, the trail enters an open, grassy meadow. The Clem Miller Environmental Center can be seen on the left. A short loop trail up Hidden Valley takes off on the right.

At the end of the meadow, the trail starts a moderately steep climb up the slopes of Inverness Ridge.

4.8   Junction #4 with the Bayview trail. Head left.

5.3   Bayview trailhead. No facilities.

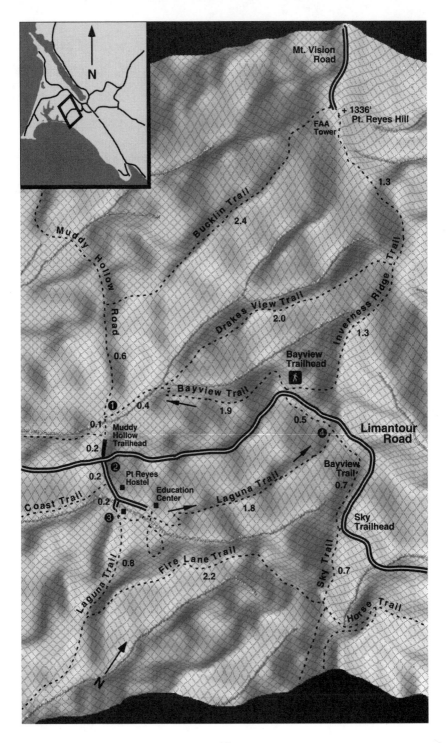

Mt. Vision
Road

+1336'
Pt. Reyes Hill

FAA
Tower

1.3

Bucklin Trail
2.4

Muddy Hollow Road

Drakes View Trail
2.0

Inverness Ridge Trail

1.3

0.6

Bayview
Trailhead

Bayview Trail
1.9

❶   0.4

0.1

Muddy
Hollow
Trailhead

0.2

0.5

❹   Limantour
Road

❷

0.2
Pt Reyes
Hostel

Education
Center

Coast Trail

0.2

Laguna Trail
1.8

Bayview
Trail

0.7

Sky
Trailhead

❸

Laguna Trail   0.8

Fire Lane Trail
2.2

Sky Trail

0.7

Horse Trail

N

48

20 Inverness Ridge - Bucklin - Bayview

Distance: 7.9 miles
Elevation Change: 1400'
Rating: Hiking - 8   Trail rocky and crowded with grasses in places.
When to Go: Good when clear, best in spring.
This is the best hike for exploring the Bishop pine forests along Inverness Ridge. It also offers great views, both east and west.

0.0 Start at the Bayview trailhead located 4.7 miles along the Limantour Road. Take the signed Inverness Ridge trail north through the gate and head downhill through coastal scrub and Bishop pine.

Up ahead, the trail levels out on an open ridgetop covered with dense coastal scrub, an ideal home for brush rabbits.

0.7 Gate. Go 100 yds. past the gate and up the paved road to pick up the trail which now climbs steeply through a Bishop pine forest.

Brush Rabbit

1.3 Junction #1. Continue straight to pass through a luxuriant mix of forest and coastal scrub that includes ceanothus, coyote bush, manzanita, oak, madrone, blackberries, coffeeberry, bracken fern, salal, monkeyflower and Bishop pine.

Up ahead, the trail enters a dense stand of tall Bishop pine with long slender trunks and few side branches. This forest is similar to the Douglas fir forests further south. Both have lots of huckleberries in the understory and both are supported by heavy, summer fog drip.

2.1 Good views. After crossing an open saddle, the trail heads steeply uphill through coastal scrub and grasses that occasionally crowd the narrow rutted path. Great views to Tomales Bay.

2.6 FAA Station and junction #2 on Point Reyes Hill at elevation 1336'. Continue along the paved road about 50 yds. to pick up the Bucklin trail which follows the green fence west, then heads downhill. The hike now rolls down a mostly open ridgeline offering great views of Drakes Bay and the headlands. In the spring, look for the white hairy star tulip.

5.0 Junction #3 with the Muddy Hollow Road. Head left.

5.6 Junction #4 with the Bayview trail. Head left and start the long easy climb towards Inverness Ridge.

7.9 Back at the trailhead. No facilities.

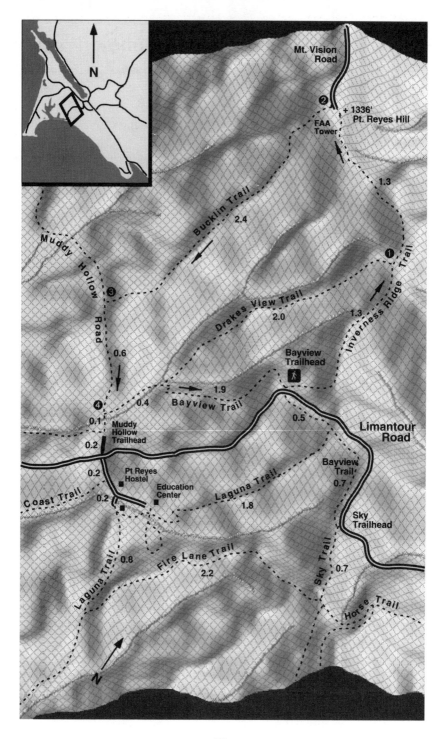

N

Mt. Vision Road

② +1336'
Pt. Reyes Hill

FAA Tower

1.3

Bucklin Trail
2.4

①

Muddy Hollow Road

③

Drakes View Trail
2.0

1.3

Inverness Ridge Trail

Bayview Trailhead

0.6

1.9

④
0.4 Bayview Trail

0.1

0.5

Limantour Road

Muddy Hollow Trailhead

0.2

Bayview Trail

Coast Trail

0.2 Pt Reyes Hostel

Education Center

Laguna Trail
1.8

0.7

0.2

Sky Trailhead

Laguna Trail

0.8

Fire Lane Trail

2.2

Sky Trail

0.7

Horse Trail

N

21 Coast - Beach - Muddy Hollow Trails

Distance: 4.8 miles
Elevation Change: 200'
Rating: Hiking - 9   Trail may be muddy when wet.
When to Go: Best in fall and winter for birds.

This hike travels along creeks, fresh and saltwater marshes and the ocean to offer a variety of habitats and good birding locations.

0.0 Park at the Muddy Hollow parking area 0.2 mile north of the Limantour Road. The hike starts by heading back up toward the road.

0.2 Limantour Road. Continue across the road towards the Hostel.

0.4 Junction #1. Before reaching the Hostel, take the Coast trail south towards Drakes Bay. The Coast trail parallels the riparian community that follows a small creek into Limantour Marsh. In the early morning, the chatter of birds fills the air. Look for Indian paintbrush, Douglas iris and buttercups in spring.

1.3 Creek crossing and alders. Up ahead, the trail skirts the marsh, then doglegs to the right towards the ocean.

2.1 Junction #2 with the beach. Take the signed trail 30' through the dunes and head right along the beach. If it's not too windy, this can be an exhilarating walk with views of Drakes Bay, refreshing ocean breakers and much beach activity. Watch for pelicans, willets and plovers. Keep an eye out for sand crabs and rock louse. On occasion, sea lions will follow your progress along the beach.

Brown Pelican

2.9 Trail inland #3. Look for the greatest concentration of people or a break in the dunes and head inland towards the Limantour parking area.

Willet

3.0 Junction, water and restroom. At the restroom, head left to pick up the Muddy Hollow trail. Look for sandpipers, willets, egrets and herons in Limantour Estero to the north.

3.4 Junction #4 with the Estero trail. Continue heading inland. The Muddy Hollow trail passes in and out of a riparian community with creeks and marshes lined with red alders.

4.8 Back at the Muddy Hollow parking area. No facilities.

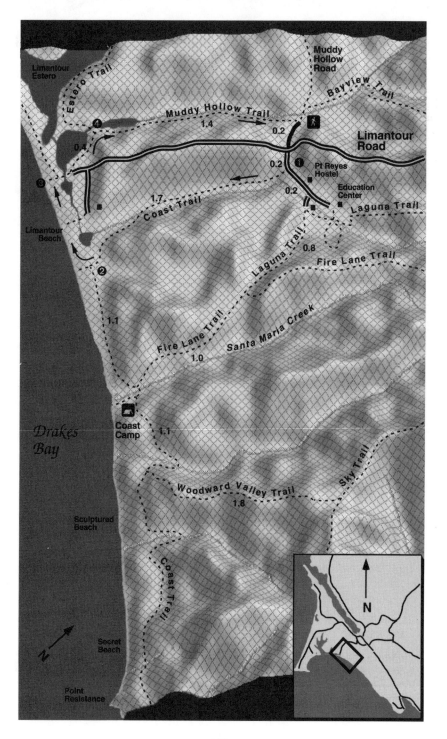

Limantour Estero

Estero Trail

Muddy Hollow Road

Bayview Trail

Muddy Hollow Trail
1.4   0.2

Limantour Road

0.4

0.2
Pt Reyes Hostel

③

0.2
Education Center

1.7   Coast Trail

Laguna Trail

Limantour Beach

②

Laguna Trail   0.8   Fire Lane Trail

1.1

Fire Lane Trail

Santa Maria Creek

1.0

Drakes Bay

Coast Camp   1.1

Sculptured Beach

Woodward Valley Trail
1.8

Sky Trail

Coast Trail

N

Secret Beach

Point Resistance

N

22 Muddy Hollow - Estero Trails

Distance: 6.4 miles
Elevation Change: 250'
Rating: Hiking - 7   Trail may be muddy and overgrown with nettles.
When to Go: Good when clear skies, best in spring, but not too wet.

This hike traverses open coast land offering excellent views of Drakes Bay, then returns via Muddy Hollow. Some parts unmaintained.

0.0 Start at the Muddy Hollow trailhead located 0.2 mile north of Limantour Road. Take the dirt road northeast through the gate.

0.1 Junction. Continue past the Bayview trail and the site of the old Muddy Hollow ranch, which was located near the Cypress trees.

In spring, iris, buttercup, cow parsnip and monkeyflower dot the open hillside. If the road is wet, look for deer tracks on the way.

0.7 Junction #1 with the Bucklin trail. Continue straight and follow the road as it heads down into the Glenbrook Creek drainage basin. You can look south to see where it enters Limantour Estero.

1.5 Junction #2. Take the Glenbrook trail left and make a short climb to a rise offering great views of the coast. As you start down a long run towards the ocean, the view of Drakes Bay keeps getting better.

2.2 Junction #3 with the Estero trail. Continue towards the ocean.

2.9 Turning point and side trip. The trail now reverses direction to head back inland. For a side trip, take the unmarked trail 0.5 mile to a point overlooking the estero.

3.7 Bridge. As you head inland, the trail drops down past eucalyptus trees. The first dairy on Point Reyes was established here in 1857 by the Steele brothers. Up ahead, the trail crosses a bridge on Glenbrook Creek. This section of trail is unmaintained and can be muddy and overgrown with stinging nettles. After crossing the bridge, the trail makes a short climb over a ridge and drops down into Muddy Hollow. The last section of trail that crosses another bridge and dam can also be overgrown. Watch out for poison oak in this last section.

5.0 Junction #4 and side trip. Take the Muddy Hollow trail to the left. For a side trip, you can go right 0.4 miles to Limantour beach.

The Muddy Hollow trail skirts a pond and then a creek that provide riparian habitat good for birding. The trail can be muddy when wet. However, it has been greatly improved since the time it was named.

6.4 Back at the Muddy Hollow trailhead. No facilities.

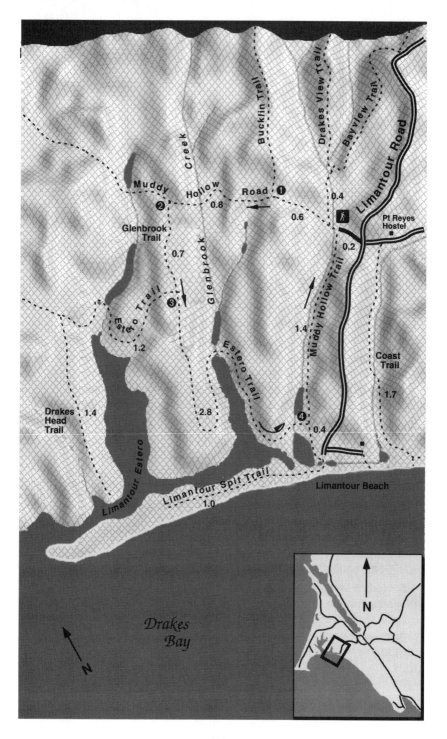

Muddy
Hollow
Road

① 0.8

② Glenbrook Trail

0.7

③

Esterio Trail
1.2

Drakes
Head
Trail   1.4

Glenbrook

Estero Trail
2.8

Creek

Bucklin Trail

Drakes View Trail

Bay view Trail

Limantour Road

0.4

Pt Reyes
Hostel

0.6

0.2

Muddy Hollow Trail

1.4

④

0.4

Coast
Trail

1.7

Limantour Estero

Limantour Spit Trail
1.0

Limantour Beach

Drakes
Bay

N

N

23 Limantour Spit - Beach Trails

Distance: 2.0 miles
Elevation Change: less than 100'
Rating: Hiking - 8   Good trail conditions.
When to Go: Anytime, best when calm and clear.

This refreshing hike along the dunes and beach provides good views, lots of birds and a reminder of the historic struggle to create a park.

0.0 Start at the Limantour parking area and head down past the restroom towards the ocean. Just after passing the marsh area, turn right and head north along the trail in the dunes.

This trail was once called Limantour Drive, which led into a subdivision called Drakes Bay Estates.This area of the development had been divided into over one hundred lots. When the National Seashore formed in 1962, six of the lots already had homes built. As you walk along, you'll see an occasional pipe or concrete pad, reminders of the heroic efforts of the early conservationists.

Modern landowners weren't the first to use this spit. Before the developers moved in, archeologists had uncovered three middens or shell mounds that were garbage dumps of the Coastal Miwoks. Not only did the middens contain shells, but archeologists also found dozens of pieces of Chinese Ming porcelain and other artifacts that indicate that Cermeno may have camped on the spit after the shipwreck of the San Agustin in 1595.

0.5 Birds of the estero. Look for egrets, herons, willets, and plovers especially in winter.

1.0 End of the road. Head west, out to the beach. To add to the hike, you can continue north 1.8 miles to the end of the spit. (You might see an old shipwreck about 1.5 miles out.) Otherwise, go left and head south back along the beach.

Harbor Seal

1.5 Harbor seal or sea lion? The two most common marine mammals at Point Reyes are harbor seals and sea lions. Harbor seals are smaller and have a mottled coat. They have large eyes and no ears. When they go under, they often sink straight down, while sea lions tend to dive forward.

Sea Lion

2.0 Limantour parking area, restrooms and water.

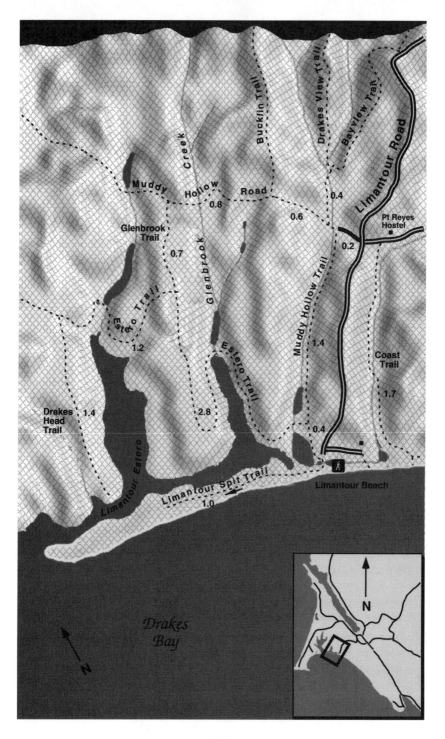

Bucklin Trail

Drakes View Trail

Bayview Trail

Limantour Road

Muddy Hollow Road

Creek

0.8

0.4

0.6

Pt Reyes Hostel

Glenbrook Trail

Glenbrook

0.7

0.2

Estero Trail

Muddy Hollow Trail

1.4

Coast Trail

1.7

1.2

Estero Trail

2.8

Drakes Head Trail

1.4

0.4

Limantour Estero

Limantour Spit Trail

1.0

Limantour Beach

Drakes Bay

N

N

24 Beach Trail to Sculptured Beach

Distance: 5.4 miles
Elevation Change: 50'
Rating: Hiking - 7   Check tide tables before taking this hike.
When to Go: Best at low tide in the summer and fall.
This hike explores the interesting rock formations and tidepools on the beaches south of Limantour.

0.0 Park in the auxiliary parking area south of the main parking lot at Limantour Beach. Take the trail across the dunes to the beach and head south. Before leaving the dunes, look back and note the trees and ranger residence, which provide a landmark for returning.

1.4 Creek and junction #1. Continue along the beach.

1.8 Santa Maria Creek and Sculptured Beach. The sandy beach here changes with the seasons. In winter, large wave action moves sand offshore lowering the level of the beach and making travel over the rocky terraces difficult. In the summer and fall, smaller wave action brings the sand back ashore and it is easier to walk along here and explore the rocks and tidepools.

2.5 Junction #2 and creek. You can climb up to a small rocky terrace and scan the beach south to Pt. Resistance. Usually, this is as far as you can go. When done exploring, retrace your steps.

If the beach sand level is high enough and there is a minus tide, you may be able to explore the beach south. You will probably have to climb down off the terrace

Low Tide

Low tide at Point Reyes occurs 37 minutes earlier than Golden Gate low tide (which is usually given in the tide tables).

Also, the tide comes in slowly at first, then rises more quickly about two hours after the minimum. You should plan to have a clear, safe route off any beach by this time.

4-6 feet to reach the beach. If you can safely do this, there are interesting caves and tunnels ahead. (This is not an approved park trail. Hike it at your own risk and be sure to watch the tide!)

3.6 Junction and Coast Camp. Head inland, veer left and follow the Coast trail towards Limantour Beach.

4.8 Junction #3. Leave the Coast trail and take the beach north.

5.3 Junction. Look for the trees and residence and head inland again.

5.4 Parking area. Restrooms and water at the main parking area.

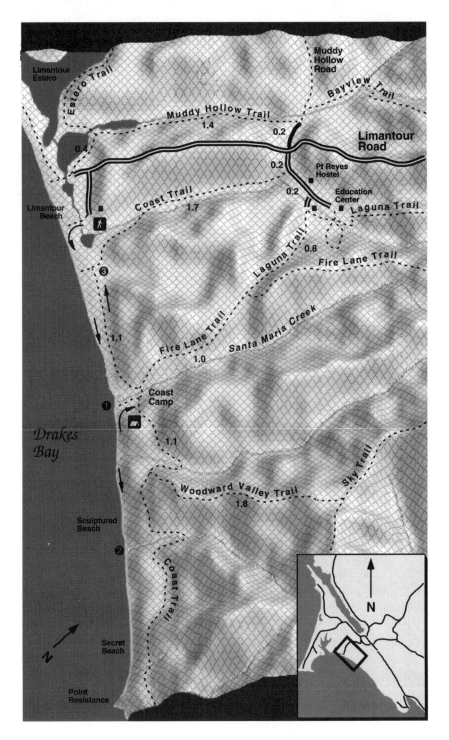

Limantour Estero

Muddy Hollow Road

Estero Trail

Bayview Trail

Muddy Hollow Trail
1.4   0.2

0.4

Limantour Road

Pt Reyes Hostel

Coast Trail
1.7

0.2

0.2

Education Center

Laguna Trail

Limantour Beach

Laguna Trail

0.8

Fire Lane Trail

❸

Santa Maria Creek

Fire Lane Trail
1.0

1.1

Coast Camp

❶

Drakes Bay

1.1

Woodward Valley Trail
1.8

Sky Trail

Sculptured Beach

❷

Coast Trail

N

Secret Beach

N

Point Resistance

25 Chimney Rock Trail

Distance: 1.6 miles
Elevation Change: less than 100'
Rating: Hiking - 10   May be muddy in wet weather.
When to Go: Best in April and May, when not too windy.

This short hike offers the best wildflower display and the most spectacular coastline views on Point Reyes.

0.0 Start at the Chimney Rock trailhead located 0.9 miles off of Sir Francis Drake Hwy. on the headlands. Follow the trail as it skirts the hillside above the cypress trees and ranger residence. The first docks on your left are for commercial fishing boats.

0.3 Junction #1 with Underhill road. Continue straight ahead. The second dock on your left was a launching pier and barracks for the US Coast Guard Lifeboat Station that operated between 1927 and 1968. Dozens of people were saved after shipwrecks on the rocks and beaches near here, including all 27 passengers and crew aboard the lumber steamer *Hartwood*.

0.4 Junction #2. Take the Overlook trail to the right.

0.5 Overlook and views. The towering 500' cliffs and storm-hewn rocks below provide treacherous sailing waters and spectacular coastline scenery. Occasionally, grey whales can be seen in winter and spring. Now retrace your steps.

SS Hartwood aground near Chimney Rock June 27, 1929

0.6 Junction. Head right towards Chimney Rock.

0.9 Chimney Rock and wildflowers. This wind-swept promontory offers one of the best wildflower displays on Point Reyes. Expert observers have counted over 60 species along the trail including hairy cat's-ears, Johnny-tuck, paintbrush, lupine, iris and checkerbloom.

(Note: The best place to see the "chimney" of Chimney Rock is from Drakes Bay Beach.) When done, head back the way you came.

1.3 Junction. Take the Underhill trail right down the grassy roadbed. If the tide is very low, there are good tidepools around the promontories to the right. Out past the second promontory is best.

1.6 Back at the trailhead with restrooms.

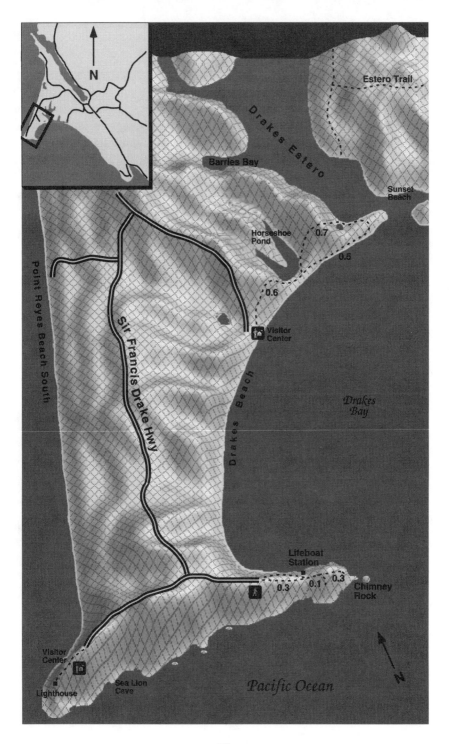

26 Drakes Beach Trail

Distance: 2.5 miles
Elevation Change: 300'
Rating: Hiking - 9 Some parts may not be passable.
When to Go: Best at low tide, good wildflowers in April and May.

This hike makes a figure-eight traveling on the beach and coastal bluffs to visit the historic marker commemorating Drake's landing.

0.0 Start at the Ken Patrick Visitor Center picnic area and take the trail left up the cliff to the bluffs above. At the top of the cliff, you have two choices. You can either follow the cliff, staying well back from the edge, or head inland to pick up a grassy-covered road heading east.

0.3 Crest. The trail reaches a high point overlooking Horseshoe Pond. Follow the road down towards the pond.

0.5 Dam and beach. As you cross the dam towards the beach, look carefully at the road coming down the hill slightly to your left. This is your return path. If the pond is too deep, you will have to traverse the small bank connecting the road to the beach. If this looks too difficult, you should return via the beach.

0.6 Beach. If the tide is not too high, continue down the beach past the cliffs and dunes to the estero.

1.1 Drakes Estero. If possible, circle the dunes and head towards the cliff and trees.

1.3 Drake's Memorial. Look for the pole and monument about 50' inland. Most experts believe that this is the spot where Drake careened the Golden Hinde for repairs in 1579. The hike continues up the road. Look for wildflowers along the bank in spring, iris, checkerbloom, Indian paintbrush and buttercups.

One of two monuments to Drake. This one is located next to the parking lot.

1.8 Horseshoe Pond. If the road across the pond is not passable, veer left and follow the fence for about 100 yds., then traverse the cliff to the beach. This is the best place to cross. The bluff is unsafe.

As you walk along the beach and terraces, look for fault lines in the cliff above. These show up as shifts in the horizontal lines.

2.5 Back at the Visitor Center.

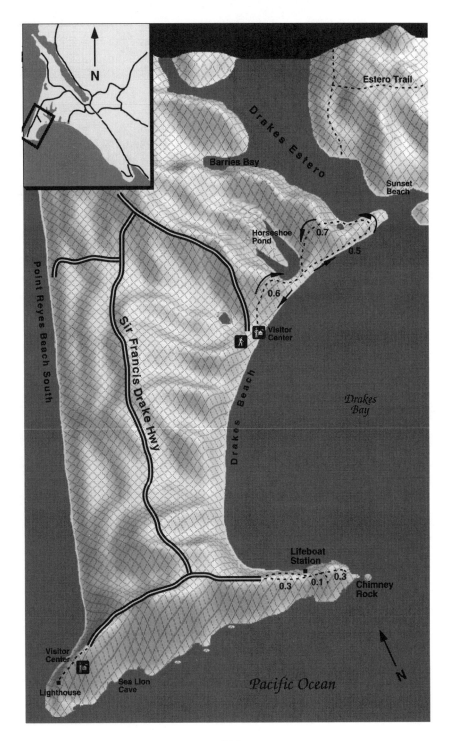

27 Estero - Drakes Head Trails

Distance: 8.8 miles
Elevation Change: 750'
Rating: Hiking - 8   Trail can be muddy in parts.
When to Go: Best in late fall and winter when calm and clear.

This is an out and back hike through rolling pastureland to the best viewpoint on Point Reyes. A good hike to see birds and mammals.

0.0 Start at the parking area off the paved road. Go through the fence and follow the Estero trail south towards the pine forest. This rangeland is part of Home Ranch which has been grazed since the 1850s. In spring, patches of deep-blue iris dot the hillsides.

1.0 Dam and bridge at point #1. Crossing the bridge of Home Bay, notice the Home Ranch farm buildings to the east. James Shafter's ranch, started in 1857, is the oldest surviving ranch on Point Reyes.

The trail now heads uphill past lupine and coyote bush. Watch for wildlife along the way - deer, rabbits, osprey, ducks and egrets.

1.5 Plateau and view of Drakes Estero. The point across the water was one of two sites called Schooner Landing. The estero and bay were deeper in earlier days allowing small schooners, like the *Point Reyes*, to deliver highly-prized butter to San Francisco.

Schooner Point Reyes

Johnson's Oyster Farm now uses the shallower estero waters.

2.4 Junction #2 with the Sunset Beach trail. Bear left, head uphill.

3.0 Junction #3 and corral. Turn right and follow the signed Drakes Head trail towards the ocean.

4.0 Water tank and trees. This is the site of the Drakes Head Ranch, which operated from the 1850s to 1960. Keep to the right.

4.4 Drakes Head. On a clear day this is the best view spot on all of Point Reyes! (Caution: The cliff edge may be unstable.) It offers a panoramic sweep of Drakes Bay from the headlands to Double Point. Look for sea lions sunning at the end of the spit. When you are ready to return, retrace your steps.

8.8 Back at the parking lot. Restrooms available.

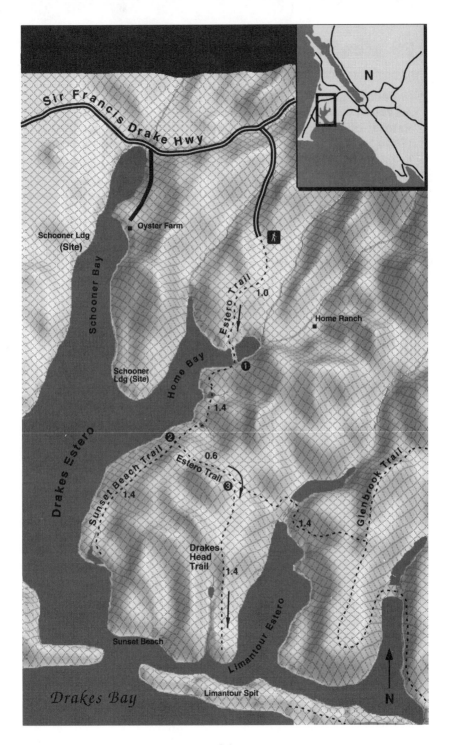

28 Beach and Lagoon Trails

Distance: 1.2 to 4.0 miles
Elevation Change: 300' for McClures and 200' for Marshall Beach.
Rating: Hiking - 8   All trails in good condition. Kehoe can be wet.
When to Go: Best weather in fall and winter, best flowers in spring.

All four of these trails provide access to great beaches on the northern end of Point Reyes. Good birding at Abbotts Lagoon.

Marshall Beach Trail - 2.4 miles

0.0 The trailhead is located 2.5 miles down the Marshall Beach Road just after the turnoff to Tomales State Park. Head north and take the trail through pastureland, then down towards a cypress grove.

1.2 Cove and beach. This picturesque beach offers sunbathing, picnicking, wading and views across Tomales Bay. If you head north along the beach, you might spot traces of a Miwok shell mound.

Abbotts Lagoon Trail - 4.0 miles

0.0 Start at the trailhead located 3.4 miles along the Pierce Point Road and head west across the open pastureland. In wet years, these fields are aglow with yellow poppies and fiddleneck.

1.5 Bridge, lagoon, wildflowers and birds. Yellow goldfields cover the hill on the left, while the bridge offers a good view spot for shore birds. Cross the bridge and follow the edge of the lagoon to the ocean.

2.0 Point Reyes Beach, also known as Ten-mile Beach.

Kehoe Beach Trail - 1.2 miles

0.0 Start at the trailhead 5.5 miles along the Pierce Point Road. This is a level trail out to the beach that parallels Kehoe Marsh. Good birding in the winter and great wildflowers in the spring.

0.6 Beach and wildflowers. The cliffs on the right are often covered in gold fields, poppies, lupine and baby blue eyes in April and May.

McClures Beach Trail - 1.2 miles (See map 29)

0.0 The trailhead is located at the end of the Pierce Point Road, 9.5 miles from the Sir Francis Drake Hwy. junction. The trail follows a ravine as it descends 300' to the ocean.

0.6 Beach. During super-low tides, there are great tidepools at the south end of the beach. Be sure to check the tide tables and plan your return while the tide is still low.

Dangerous Surf! Do not swim or wade on these ocean beaches.

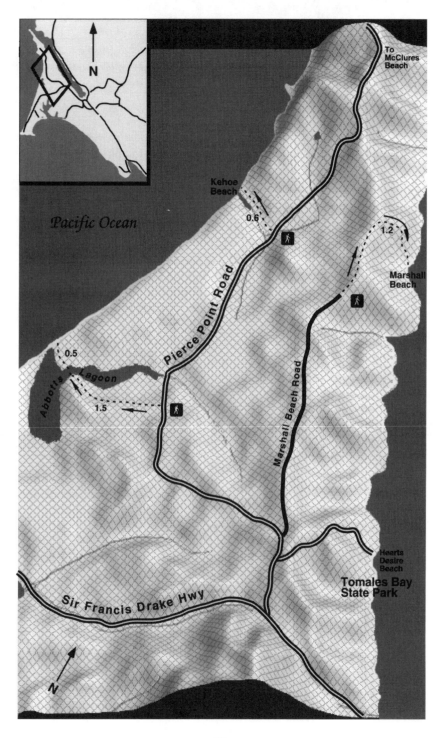

Pacific Ocean

To McClures Beach

Kehoe Beach

0.6

1.2

Marshall Beach

0.5

Abbott's Lagoon

1.5

Pierce Point Road

Marshall Beach Road

Hearts Desire Beach

Tomales Bay State Park

Sir Francis Drake Hwy

N

N

29 Tomales Point Trail

Distance: 9.4 miles
Elevation Change: 1000'
Rating: Hiking - 9   Trail conditions good.
When to Go: Winter is good; best flowers in April and May.

This hike along an open, exposed ridge can be spectacular or miserable depending on the weather. Carry ponchos in case of fog.

0.0 Start at the parking lot at the end of the Pierce Point Road. Follow the signs around the old dairy ranch. If fog cuts your hike short, you can tour the ranch when you get back.

0.8 Point #1 with spectacular coastal views. Just before the trail turns inland, you can see the dramatic coastal cliffs to the north rising over 400' above the ocean. In spring, this spot also provides a great wildflower display with yellow gold fields, tidy tips, buttercups, sun cups, poppies, lupine and wild strawberries.

1.0 The trail heads inland offering a view east down White Gulch to Hog Island in Tomales Bay.

Watch for Tule elk and for their large V-shaped tracks on the trail.

2.5 Highest point at 471'. As you climb to the highest spot on Pierce Point, you can see across Bodega Bay to the Bodega headlands and the Sonoma coast. On clear days, look for the jutting profile of Mt. Saint Helena 30 miles northeast.

Tule Elk

3.3 Lower Pierce Ranch site and unmarked junction #2. At the ravine, near the cypress trees, a small trail heads right down the right side of the ravine to a beach on Tomales Bay. Continue on the main trail.

4.0 Bird Rock viewpoint. If the tide is right, you can see a blowhole on the left side of the rock. From here, the trail climbs through a sandy area and dunes.

4.7 Tomales Point. In 1852, the English merchant ship, *Oxford*, mistaking Tomales Bay for San Francisco Bay, came full sail into the bay until she ran permanently aground just before Hog Island. After enjoying the view, retrace your steps back south.

9.4 Back at Pierce Point trailhead. Restrooms available.

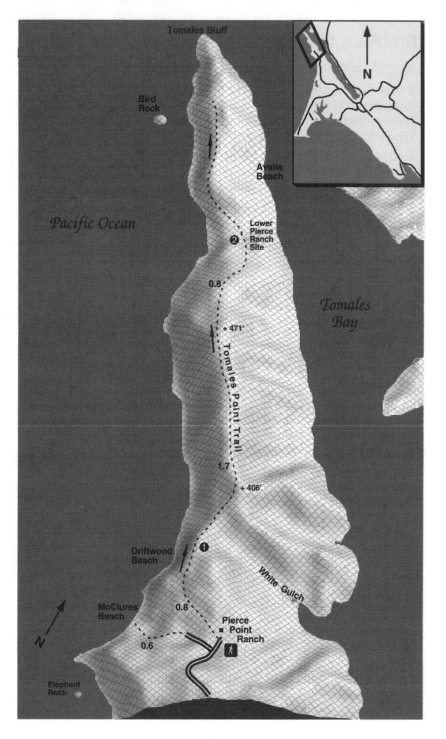

Tomales Bluff

Bird
Rock

Pacific Ocean

Avalis
Beach

Lower
Pierce
Ranch
Site

❷

0.8

+ 471'

Tomales Point Trail

Tomales
Bay

1.7

+ 406'

Driftwood
Beach

❶

White Gulch

McClures
Beach

0.8

Pierce
Point
Ranch

N

0.6

Elephant
Rock

N

30 Five Brooks Trailhead to Bear Valley

Distance: 4.6 miles
Elevation Change: 200'
Rating: Hiking - 8   The trail can be very muddy or very dusty.
When to Go: Best in winter and spring, but not when wet.

This one-way hike explores the terrain of the San Andreas rift zone. Vegetation includes forest, meadow, pasture and wildflowers.

Shuttle Hike. Leave pickup cars at Bear Valley and shuttle all hikers to the Five Brooks parking area and trailhead.

0.0 Go through the gate and heads west towards Inverness Ridge.

0.1 Junction. Continue past the Rift Zone trail. (It's often too muddy.)

0.2 Junction #1. Take the Stewart trail right towards the south.

0.3 Junction. Go through the metal gate and head downhill towards the Rift Zone trail. California hazelnut dominates the understory here. At the bottom of the hill continue straight through a 4-way junction to a meadow, then head left to cross the creek.

0.4 Creek. At the creek, take the signed Rift Zone trail left.

1.4 Private property. A sign indicates that the trail is now crossing land owned by the Vedanta Society, a religious retreat organization.

3.1 Junction #2. Go through the gate, head right 100' and then left across the pasture. Up ahead, look for a glimpse of the Vedanta retreat house about one-half mile on your left. This magnificent old Victorian, called "The Oaks", was solidly built out of redwood by James Shafter in 1869 and easily survived the 1906 earthquake. James Shafter, and his brother, Oscar, two lawyers from Vermont, at one time owned most of the Point Reyes peninsula.

The Oaks c. 1920s

4.0 Road. The hike passes through two gates and crosses the main road to the Vedanta house. The area before the gates can be very muddy if cows have churned up the soil. After passing through the second gate, the trail skirts a marshy area, climbs a knoll, then drops into a meadow leading to Bear Valley.

4.6 Bear Valley trailhead.

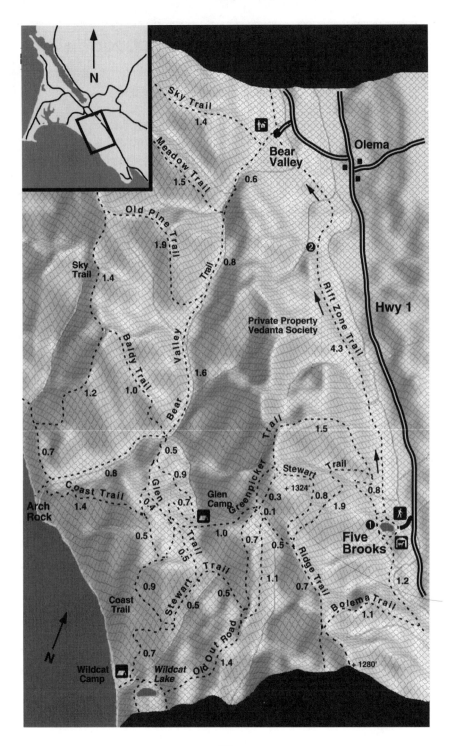

N

Sky Trail
1.4

Meadow Trail
1.5

Old Pine Trail
1.9

Sky Trail
1.4

Bear Valley

Olema

Hwy 1

0.6

0.8

❷

Rift Zone Trail
4.3

Private Property
Vedanta Society

Baldy Trail
1.0

1.2

Bear Valley Trail
1.6

1.5

0.7

0.5

Stewart Trail

0.8

Coast Trail

0.8

0.9

+1324'

0.3

0.8

1.9

0.8

Arch Rock

1.4

Glen Trail
0.4

0.7

Glen Camp

Greenpicker Trail

0.1

❶

Five Brooks

0.5

1.0

0.7

0.5

1.1

Ridge Trail

1.2

0.9

Stewart Trail
0.5

0.5

Coast Trail

0.7

Wildcat Camp

Wildcat Lake

Old Out Road
1.4

0.7

Bolema Trail
1.1

+1280'

N

70

31 Kehoe Beach to Abbotts Lagoon

Distance: 5.1 miles - includes 2 miles on the beach
Elevation Change: 100'
Rating: Hiking - 7   Trail can be wet near the marsh.
When to Go: Best in April and May when not too windy.

This one-way trail and beach hike is one of the three best wildflower hikes on Point Reyes. It's best in morning before winds get too strong.

Shuttle Hike. Leave pickup cars at Abbotts Lagoon trailhead, 3.4 miles along the Pierce Point Road and shuttle hikers another 2.1 miles to the Kehoe Beach trailhead.

0.0 The trail starts next to an exposed slab of Monterey shale on the northern hillside and follows a mostly level path through sandy soil to the beach. On the left, Kehoe Marsh provides freshwater habitat for sedges, reeds and birds. In spring, the grassy hills on the right are dotted with fragrant bush lupine and occasional patches of iris.

0.5 Dunes, cliffs and wildflowers. Take the narrow path towards the right along the exposed cliff to view gold fields, poppies, tidy tips, baby blue eyes and blue lupine.

At the beach, head down by the water and hike along the wet sand south towards Abbotts Lagoon.

Gold Fields

3.1 Abbotts Lagoon. You should be able to spot the lagoon from the beach by looking for the low-lying opening in the dunes. The lagoon is close to the ocean and low enough in elevation that heavy breakers enter it at high tide and create brackish water. Follow the northern edge of the lagoon inland. Look for lupine and lizard tail along the way.

3.6 Bridge and wildflowers. Cross the bridge and enjoy another hillside covered in gold. Just like Chimney Rock and Kehoe Beach, the best wildflower displays often appear in the most hostile environments. Up ahead, notice the wind-pruned coastal scrub on the hillside opposite the lagoon. Also, keep an eye out for birds.

Continue following the trail as it heads inland to the east. After crossing a small swale, the trail passes through fields of poppies, lupine, mustard and orange fiddleneck.

5.1 Abbotts Lagoon trailhead with pickup cars and restrooms.

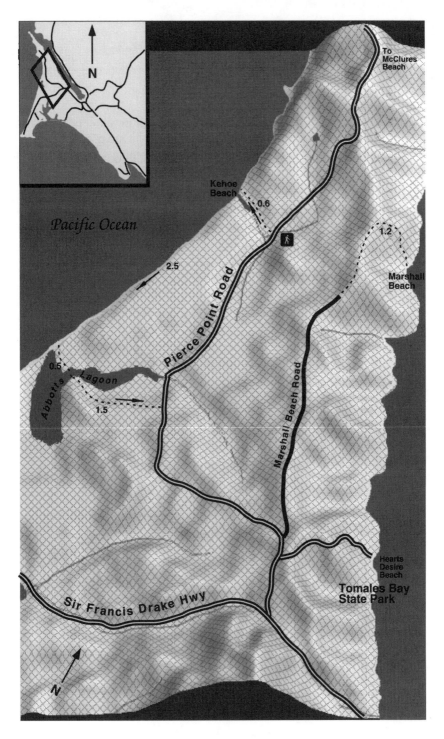

Pacific Ocean

To McClures Beach

Kehoe Beach   0.6

1.2

Marshall Beach

2.5

Pierce Point Road

0.5

Abbotts Lagoon

1.5

Marshall Beach Road

Hearts Desire Beach

Tomales Bay State Park

Sir Francis Drake Hwy

N

N

32 Olema Valley to Five Brooks

Distance: 5.5 miles
Elevation Change: 600'
Rating: Hiking - 9   Trail can have standing water in wet conditions.
When to Go: Excellent anytime, best when the hills are green.

This one-way hike meanders, like the local creeks, through a mixture of vegetation along the San Andreas fault zone.

Shuttle Hike. Leave pickup cars at Five Brooks and shuttle all hikers to the Olema Valley trailhead at milemarker 18.17, north of Dogtown.

0.0 The trail starts in a meadow and heads northwest with good views to Inverness Ridge to the west. The "Hazardous Conditions Ahead" sign refers to a marshy area and creek crossing that can result in 1-2" of standing water in wet times (more if raining).

0.4 Junction #1 with the Teixeira trail. Continue north past grasses and tall deadly nightshade with flower heads in an umbrella shape.

0.8 Creek crossings. The trail crosses Pine Gulch Creek which follows an old faultline on its way to Bolinas Lagoon.

1.6 Earthquake country. Rolling hills, sag ponds, small scarps (slides) and slumps provide topographic evidence of the thousands of earthquakes that have formed the Olema Valley rift zone through geological time.

This variety of terrain supports a variety of vegetation. Alders line the creeks. Douglas fir and bay trees compete for light along the moist hillsides. Meadows, dotted with coyote bush and coffeeberry, offer good views to the surrounding hills.

2.7 Junction #2 with a spur trail to the highway and the Randall trail. Continue north. If the trail is damp, look for animal tracks in the sandy soil. Up ahead, the trail climbs to another spur trail and better views.

4.0 Junction #3 with the Bolema trail. This is the highest point on the hike at 700'. Bear right and start a moderately steep descent through dense cover of Douglas fir, ferns, hazelnut, vines and nettles.

4.8 Small bridge. Up ahead, the creek widens into a broad, flat streambed shaded by a thicket of alders and bays.

5.2 Junction. The trail to the right heads to the stables. Continue left to circle the lake clockwise.

5.3 Junction #4. Bear right to skirt the lake back to the trailhead.

5.5 Five Brooks trailhead. Pickup cars, tables, water and restrooms.

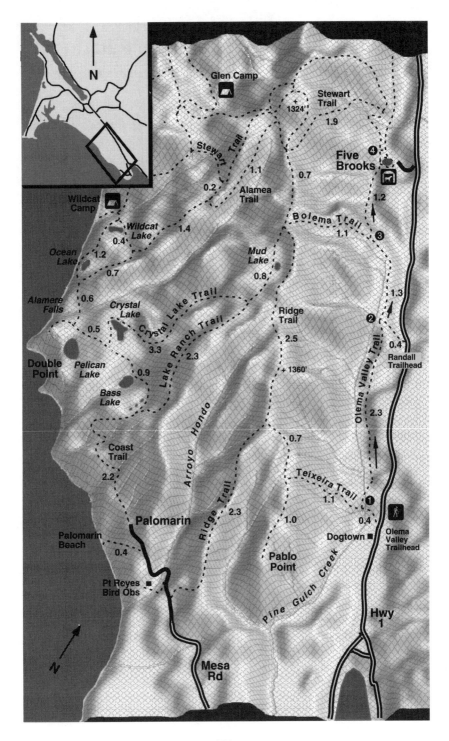

33 Olema Valley Trailhead to Palomarin

Distance: 6.9 miles
Elevation Change: 1100'
Rating: Hiking - 8   Trail can be wet and muddy at the start.
When to Go: Good anytime when not too wet.
This hike provides a good climb through dense forest, then great views at Pablo Point before descending to the Bird Observatory.

Shuttle Hike. Leave passengers at the Olema Valley trailhead at milemarker 18.17, just north of Dogtown and deliver pickup cars to the Point Reyes Bird Observatory Field Station along Mesa Road. Return drivers to the trailhead.

0.0 Start out heading north across the meadow. The trail can be muddy and wet in the marshy areas.

0.3 Creek. Pine Gulch Creek usually can be forded on small rocks.

0.4 Junction #1. Take the Teixeira trail left towards Pablo Point. This is the last of the marshy areas. The heavily rutted Teixeira trail makes a moderately steep climb to the forested Inverness Ridge.

1.5 Junction #2 with Pablo Point trail. You can cut the hike short by 2 miles by heading north here, otherwise head south for Pablo Point.

2.5 Pablo Point at 840'. Pablo Point offers a sweeping panorama of Stinson Beach, Bolinas Lagoon and the southern coastline. Towards the east, across the Olema Valley, Bolinas Ridge provides an interesting backdrop. When you are ready to continue, retrace your steps northwards.

3.5 Junction with the Teixeira trail. Continue north towards the Ridge trail and the trail to Palomarin.

4.2 Junction #3. This broad landing under a canopy of overhanging bay and tanoak trees is the highest point on the hike at 1140'. Head south towards Palomarin. Up ahead, the forest becomes darker and more dense as it changes from older to younger Douglas fir trees.

5.2 Good views. The flora changes to coastal scrub and small firs allowing good views east to Pablo Point and Bolinas Lagoon. When you head downhill more steeply, look for spring wildflowers, starting with iris in late January.

6.5 Junction #4 with Mesa Road. Head right.

6.9 Point Reyes Bird Observatory Field Station near Palomarin and waiting cars. If you have time, visit the small museum.

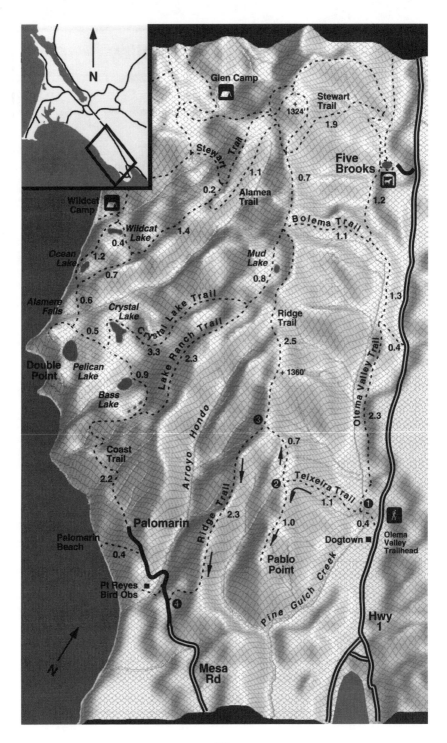

34 Sky Trailhead to Bear Valley

Distance: 7.1 miles
Elevation Change: 750' up and 1300' down
Rating: Hiking - 10   Good trail conditions.
When to Go: Excellent anytime, best when clear.

This is the easist and best all-around hike for exploring the forested Inverness Ridge and Bear Valley. Good views too.

Shuttle Hike. Leave pickup cars at Bear Valley and shuttle all hikers to the Sky trailhead about 3.5 miles along the Limantour Road.

0.0 The Sky trail starts by heading south up an old ranch road.

0.7 Junction #1. Take the Horse trail left through dense vegetation along the moist, north-facing slope of Mt. Wittenberg. Up ahead, the trail circles a landslide that occurred in 1982.

1.1 Junction #2. Turn right and head uphill on the Mt. Wittenberg trail.

1.8 Junction #3 and more views. The grassy slopes of Mt. Wittenberg and Sky Camp below provide a picturesque foreground to Drakes Bay and the Point Reyes headlands. Take the Mt. Wittenberg trail left up to the top. Look for tidy tips and lupine in May and June.

2.0 Mt. Wittenberg at 1407' is the highest spot on Point Reyes. Retrace your steps down the mountain when ready to continue.

2.2 Junction. Take the Sky trail southwest, down along the ridge line.

2.6 Two junctions #4. Continue south on the Sky trail which now enters a magnificent forest of Douglas fir towering over a smaller forest of elderberry. In early spring, the light-green leaves of the elderberry provide a striking contrast to the darker colors of the fir. Later in spring, cream-colored blossoms and inedible red berries create changing patterns in this woodsy setting.

Red Elderberry

3.3 Junction and meadow. The Woodward Valley trail heads right through a beauatiful meadow ideal for picnics. Continue straight along the ridgetop.

3.6 Junction #5. Take the Old Pine trail left as it leaves the Inverness Ridge and makes a long, gradual descent down to Bear Valley.

5.5 Junction #6 and Divide Meadow. Head downhill to the left.

7.1 Bear Valley trailhead with water, restrooms and Visitor Center.

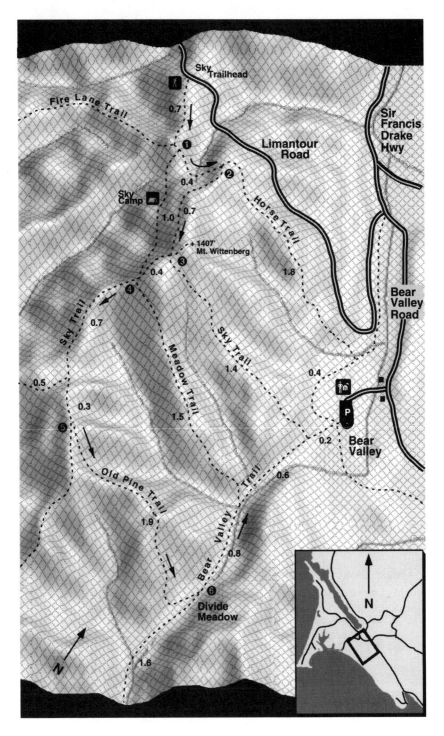

Sky Trailhead

Fire Lane Trail

Limantour Road

Sir Francis Drake Hwy

0.7

①

0.4 ②

Sky Camp

Horse Trail

1.0 0.7

+ 1407' Mt. Wittenberg

0.4 ③

④

0.7

Sky Trail

Bear Valley Road

0.5

0.3

Sky Trail

1.4

Meadow Trail

1.5

0.4

P

Bear Valley

⑤

Old Pine Trail

0.2

Bear Valley Trail

0.6

1.9

0.8

⑥ Divide Meadow

N

1.6

N

78

A1 A Selection of Best Trails

Not sure where to go? Here is our selection of best trails. Remember that the season and weather strongly influence trail conditions.

The 3 Best Wildflower Trails
1. Chimney Rock, Hike 25
2. Kehoe Beach and Abbotts Lagoon trails, Hikes 28 and 31
3. Either Tomales Pt., Hike 29 or the Coast trail, Hikes 6 and 15

The 3 Best Creek and Waterfall Trails
1. Bear Valley, Hike 4
2. Alamere Falls, an extension of Hike 13
3. Fern Canyon Nature trail at PRBO, Hike 12

The 3 Best View Trails
1. Drakes Head, Hike 27
2. Double Point, Hike 13
3. Either Chimney Rock, Hike 25 or the Coast trail, Hikes 6 and 7

The 3 Best Birding Trails
1. Limantour Spit, Hike 24
2. Muddy Hollow trail, Hikes 21 and 22
3. The Bird Observatory area, Hike 12

The 3 Best Flora Trails
1. Bear Valley, Hikes 2, 3, and 4
2. Inverness Ridge, Hikes 6 and 7
3. Greenpicker trail, Hikes 9 and 10

The 3 Best Beginner Trails
1. Bear Valley trail, Hike 4
2. Bear Valley and Inverness Ridge trails, Hike 3
3. Bear Valley Interpretative trails, Hike 1

The 3 Best Beaches or Beach Trails
1. Drakes Beach and Hike 26
2. Limantour Beach and Hike 24
3. Sculptured Beach and Hike 23 (low tide only)

The 3 Best Foggy Day Trails
1. Bear Valley, Hike 4
2. Olema Valley and Inverness Ridge, Hike 8
3. Bear Valley and Inverness Ridge, Hike 3

A2 A Trail for All Seasons

December - January

The sun is at its lowest angle of the year and it's often cold and wet. But now you can discover one of the great secrets of Point Reyes. Head for the coast where it can be warm and sunny, especially during foggy days inland. Now is also the time for whale watching and for discovering migrating winter birds. Hikes 12, 13, 14 and 21 through 29 are all good choices.

February - March

This is great hiking time. Water runoff is high. The whales are heading north. Milkmaids, hound's tongue and Douglas iris start the wildflower parade. If the coast is clear, go there first, especially the south-facing areas. Otherwise head inland. Good hikes include 4, 13, 14, 15, 25 and 27.

April - May

This is the premier hiking time of the year. The hills are gloriously green and wildflowers are peaking. If it's not foggy or windy, be sure to try one of the coastal wildflower areas, either Tomales Point, Chimney Rock, Drakes Head or Abbotts Lagoon. All of the hikes are great, especially Hikes 6, 15, 25, 29 and 31.

June - July

While summer fog can make the coast cold and miserable, fog drip on the Inverness Ridge can provide a welcome relief to the hot interior. Some summer wildflowers, monkeyflower, poppy, yarrow and clarkia, hang on while the hills turn brown. Hikes 3, 8, 9, 10 and 33.

August - September

Now is the time to avoid the dry, dusty roads. Let the weather be your guide. Try the coast first, then the ridges. Head for north-facing trails, creeks, conifer forests and ripe huckleberries. Hikes 4, 5, 9, 10, 28 and 33.

October - November

Look for fall colors from poison oak, big leaf maple and California black oak. First winter storms can mean gusty winds, clear days and marvelous views. It's a good time for coastal trails, beaches and tidepools. Hikes 4, 12, 21, 23, 26, 28 and 31.

A3 Backpacking Camps

There are four backcamping camps at Point Reyes. These campgrounds are free of charge. However, a camping permit is required. Permits are available at the Visitor Center and reservations for them can be made up to two months in advance. Reservations are almost always necessary for summer, holidays and weekends - phone 415-663-1092.

All camp sites have water, restrooms, tables and charcoal grills. No wood gathering is allowed. All campgrounds have metal poles for hanging food packs. There are no bears, but raccoons are plentiful. There is very little shade at any of the camps, so be prepared for sun, wind or fog.

The safest overnight parking is at the Visitor Center at Bear Valley. However, do not leave valuables in the car anywhere. All of the camps are accessible by bicycle on designated trails.

Sky Camp

Sky Camp has 12 sites and is located on the grassy slopes of Mt. Wittenberg, 1020' above sea level. It has the most secluded individual camp sites and offers the best views, especially of Drakes Bay and the headlands.

The shortest route to Sky Camp is 1.2 miles starting from the Sky trailhead, see Hike 18. The best medium distance hike from Bear Valley is via the Old Pine trail, a distance of 5.4 miles along Hike 3.

The bicycle route to Sky Camp starts from the Sky trailhead, Hike 18.

Coast Camp

Coast Camp has 14 sites and is located just south of Limantour Beach at an elevation of 100'. It offers easy access to Sculptured Beach (pick up a tide book at the Visitor Center). Some sites are exposed to strong northwest winds.

The shortest route to Coast Camp is 1.5 miles from Limantour Beach, see Hike 24. The best route from Bear Valley lies along the Old Pine and Woodward Valley trails, 6.7 miles. Start out on Hike 3, then switch over to Hike 6 at the Woodward Valley junction.

The bike route starts from the Muddy Hollow area, see Hike 22.

Glen Camp

Glen Camp has 12 sites and is located in a small meadow at an elevation of 600'. It is the most isolated and secluded of the four backpacking camps and some sites are shaded.

The best route to Glen Camp starts from Bear Valley and is 4.6 miles along Hike 7. If you want more climbing, you can start from Five Brooks and hike the Stewart trail over Firtop at 1324', then take the Greenpicker trail for a total distance of 5.0 miles, see Hike 9.

The bicycle route to Glen Camp is along the Stewart trail to the Glen trail, then the Glen Camp Loop trail, start on Hike 9.

Wildcat Camp

Wildcat Camp has 12 sites and is located in an open grassy meadow just above Wildcat Beach. It offers easy access to the beach and Alamere Falls. It is about two miles from Double Point.

The easist route to Wildcat Camp is to hike 5.5 miles north along the Coast trail from Palomarin, see Hike 14. From Bear Valley, you can start on Hike 7 and hike a total of 6.3 miles to Wildcat Camp. You can also reach the camp from Five Brooks by starting out on Hike 9 and hiking a total distance of 5.7 miles.

The bicycle route follows the Stewart trail, see hike 9.

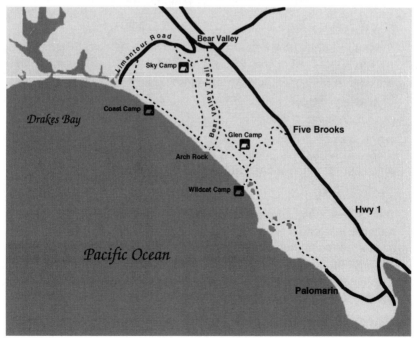

A4 Northern Beaches

McClures Beach

McClures Beach is the most scenic of the north section beaches. It is a sandy beach, almost a mile long, with large granite cliffs blocking the ends. It is a great beach for picnicking and watching waves.

At low tide, you can climb through a slot in the cliffs at the south end of the beach to explore a smaller beach and tidepools.

Kehoe Beach

Kehoe Beach is at the north end of a long beach with three names: Great Beach, Ten-Mile Beach or Point Reyes Beach. At low tide, you can explore the beach north. There are good tidepools past the rocky area which may be difficult to cross.

Abbotts Lagoon

Abbotts Lagoon is known for its winter birds, spring wildflowers, summer winds and fall canoeing. Canoes should be portaged from the road about one mile north of the main parking area.

Point Reyes Beaches, North and South

These two sandy beaches are in the middle of the Great Beach. They are easily accessible with parking located just 100 yds. away. These beaches have abundant driftwood and are great for long walks.

Chimney Rock

This beach is rocky and only used for tidepooling. You can access the beach near the Rescue Station, then head southwest towards the ocean. The best tidepools are located past the second prominence, which can only be reached at low tide.

Drakes Bay

This is the best all-around beach at Point Reyes. Its orientation protects it from large ocean waves and the tall cliffs provide some shelter from summer winds. The beach is great for walking, picnicking and wading.

The Visitor Center has a small aquarium and exhibits. The Visitor Center and cafe are open daily.

Marshall Beach

This beach is located on Tomales Bay where both air and water temperature are warmer. Swimming is possible.

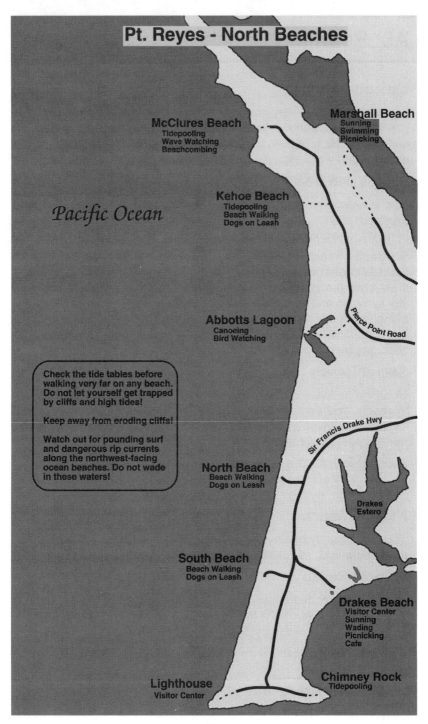

Pt. Reyes - North Beaches

McClures Beach
Tidepooling
Wave Watching
Beachcombing

Marshall Beach
Sunning
Swimming
Picnicking

Kehoe Beach
Tidepooling
Beach Walking
Dogs on Leash

Pacific Ocean

Abbotts Lagoon
Canoeing
Bird Watching

Pierce Point Road

Check the tide tables before
walking very far on any beach.
Do not let yourself get trapped
by cliffs and high tides!

Keep away from eroding cliffs!

Watch out for pounding surf
and dangerous rip currents
along the northwest-facing
ocean beaches. Do not wade
in these waters!

Sir Francis Drake Hwy

North Beach
Beach Walking
Dogs on Leash

Drakes
Estero

South Beach
Beach Walking
Dogs on Leash

Drakes Beach
Visitor Center
Sunning
Wading
Picnicking
Cafe

Lighthouse
Visitor Center

Chimney Rock
Tidepooling

A5 Southern Beaches

Limantour Beach

Limantour Beach is very popular for picnicking, wading and walking. If you walk towards the north end, look for remains of a shipwreck in the sand about 1/2 mile from the spit. The nearby estero and marshes are good for bird watching.

Sculptured Beach

This is one of the most interesting beaches on Point Reyes. It is best explored at low tide when the sedimentary layers of the marine terrace are exposed.

Sculptured Beach changes with the seasons as moving sand varies the relationship of the sandy beach to the rocks. At times, usually in the winter, the sand is low, making the beach almost impassable. In the summer and fall, the sand is higher and you can almost stroll along until you reach a small promontory, where you have to climb down 4-6 feet to continue. If you can get past this point, the beach becomes even more interesting with caves, tunnels and tidepools.

Secret Beach

Of all the beaches on this map, Secret Beach is the most difficult one to reach. You can only access it at minus tide and low surf. Even then, it may involve some significant climbing and wading. The only route is past Sculptured Beach (as described above).

Secret Beach itself is a sandy beach about one mile long, ending at Pt. Resistance. Do not plan to stay on Secret Beach for long. You need to return during low tide.

Kelham Beach

This small sandy beach lies between Pt. Resistance and Arch Rock. At very low tide, you can explore the sea tunnel under Arch Rock.

Wildcat Beach

This is a sandy beach two miles long with Alamere Falls at one end. The beach can easily be walked except during high tide. However, you do have to hike at least four miles to get there.

Palomarin Beach

Palomarin Beach is mostly a rocky beach with some marine terraces that can be explored at low tide.

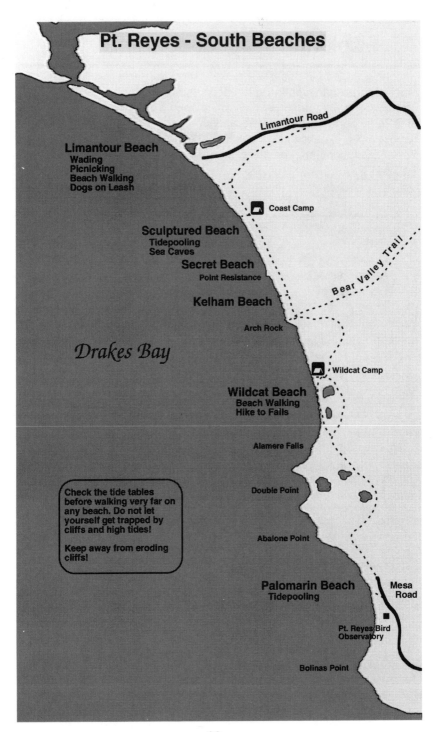

Pt. Reyes - South Beaches

Limantour Beach
Wading
Picnicking
Beach Walking
Dogs on Leash

Limantour Road

Coast Camp

Sculptured Beach
Tidepooling
Sea Caves

Bear Valley Trail

Secret Beach
Point Resistance

Kelham Beach

Arch Rock

Drakes Bay

Wildcat Camp

Wildcat Beach
Beach Walking
Hike to Falls

Alamere Falls

Double Point

Check the tide tables
before walking very far on
any beach. Do not let
yourself get trapped by
cliffs and high tides!

Keep away from eroding
cliffs!

Abalone Point

Palomarin Beach
Tidepooling

Mesa
Road

Pt. Reyes Bird
Observatory

Bolinas Point

A6 Exploring Tidepools

Most of the organisms living in tidepools are invertebrates; they have no backbone. Instead, they have developed an exoskeleton to protect their body parts from predators and crashing surf. For example, crabs have a chitin exoskeleton; mussels have a shell of calcium carbonate. Some exceptions are sea stars, anemones, nudibranchs and fish.

The intertidal habitat can be divided into four zones as shown below.

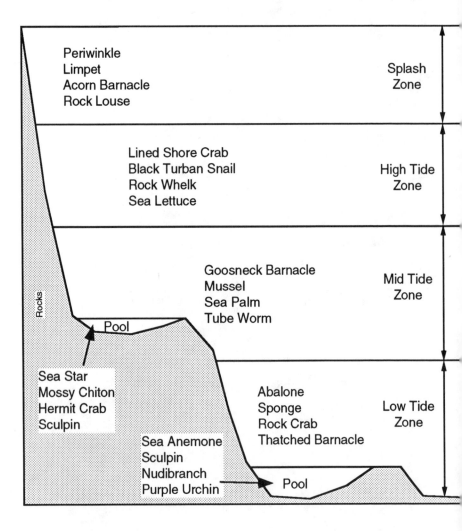

87

Guidelines for exploring tidepools.

- Check the tide tables and plan your trip accordingly.
- Beaches are often windy. Dress with warm layers.
- Tidepool rocks are slippery. Wear tennis shoes or rubber boots.
- Bring a change of clothes in case you get wet.
- The lower you get, the more you'll see.
- Check under rocks, but always replace them like you found them.
- If you pick a critter up, put it back in the same place.

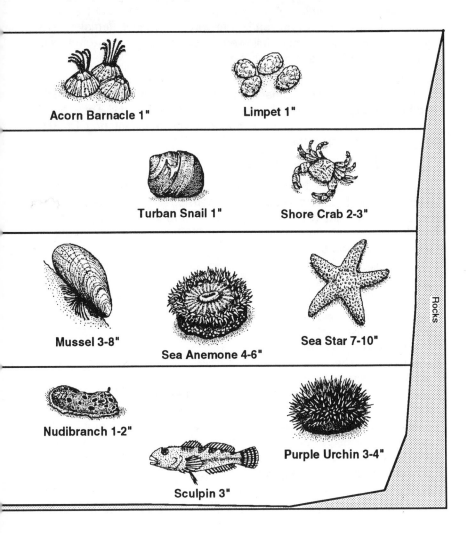

Acorn Barnacle 1"

Limpet 1"

Turban Snail 1"

Shore Crab 2-3"

Mussel 3-8"

Sea Anemone 4-6"

Sea Star 7-10"

Nudibranch 1-2"

Purple Urchin 3-4"

Sculpin 3"

Rocks

A7 Whales and Whalewatching

Each winter, more than 15,000 California grey whales pass Point Reyes on their 6000 mile journey southward to breed in the warm lagoons of Baja California. These whales hug the coastline, often passing within one-quarter mile of the Point Reyes lighthouse and other coastal prominences.

When to Watch

The southward migration of the grey whale begins at Point Reyes in December and peaks in early January. Pregnant females are generally the first to arrive, followed by courtship groups (often two males and one female) and then the adolescents.

The northerly return trip begins passing Point Reyes in early March and is led by newly pregnant females. Newborn young and their mothers arrive later, usually between April and June. They often travel slowly and very close to shore, sometimes entering Drakes Bay, providing a memorable view.

The California Grey Whale

Grey whales almost became extinct during the early 1900s. Their migration and breeding habits made them easy targets for Russian, Japanese and American whaling ships. Fortunately, with protection established along the west coast in 1946, they have made a remarkable comeback.

The California grey whale is a baleen whale with rows of long fingernail-like plates (baleen) in the roof of its mouth. These plates are used to filter krill, plankton and other

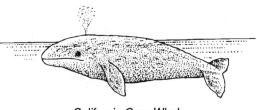

California Grey Whale

crustaceans from the rich Arctic waters, where they do most of their feeding. One researcher reported that a young female in captivity consumed over 1800 pounds of squid a day, gaining weight at the rate of 2 pounds per hour. Adult males can reach a length of 50 feet and weigh over 30 tons. A new born calf enters the world about the size of a compact car, weighing up to a ton.

Baleen whales have two blowholes in their head where they spout water 10 - 15 feet high. The spout is the most conspicuous sign of the grey whale and lasts from 5-10 seconds. Following the spout, you can often see the tail fluke as the whale heads down for a dive of 20 seconds to 2 minutes.

Where To Go

The Point Reyes lighthouse, 240 feet above the ocean, is the best place to see migrating whales. However, even though the lighthouse is well above sea level, it is still 300 steps below the clifftop. These stairs are open from 10am to 4pm, Thursday through Monday, weather permitting. A small Visitor Center sits atop the bluff, 0.4 miles from the parking area. You can check on whale activity in the Visitor Center before you make the trek down the steps. However, the historic lighthouse itself is well worth a look. Check for the times of ranger-led tours.

Point Reyes Lighthouse

During peak months, usually January and February, between 10am and 2pm, the park service restricts traffic to the lighthouse and provides parking and a shuttle bus at the North Beach parking area, three miles away.

Although the lighthouse is only about 20 miles from the main Visitor Center at Bear Valley, it takes about 45 minutes driving time.

What To Bring

Ideally, the weather will be sunny and calm and you'll see half a dozen whales per hour. However, you can't count on either condition. Bring warm clothing in case of fog and wind. Also, binoculars are essential. Wide-angle binoculars are best, so you can spot whales quickly. Telescopes don't work well because of narrow fields of view.

Other Places to See Whales

Other viewpoints for whalewatching include Double Point (see Hike 13), the Coast trail above Miller Point (see Hike 6) and the Coast trail just north of Palomarin (see Hike 13 or 15).

Other Whales

Two other species of whales that might be seen along the coast include the blue and the humpback whales. Blue whales are the largest creatures on earth, about twice the size of the grey whale and are occasionally seen from May to September. Humpback whales are sometimes seen in August or September.

A8 Animals and Animal Tracks

Imagine a land abundant with grizzly and black bears, mountain lions, tule elk, deer and coyotes. All evidence suggests that Point Reyes was rich in wild life when Drake landed in 1578. Now, the bears are gone, incompatible with humans and cattle. The coyotes may be returning. Possibly, one or two mountain lions remain and the tule elk, once extinct, are again thriving. The only large mammal to continuously inhabit the land is the mule deer.

Tule Elk

Tule Elk

It is estimated that most of the Tule elk vanished by the 1850s, victims of hunters. The elk were reintroduced in 1978 and are confined to 2600 acres along the northern end of the Point Reyes peninsula. Usually the herd of 90 or so animals is split into two or three smaller herds. The best way to see them is to hike the Pierce Point trail, Hike 23.

Deer

Point Reyes has three species of deer, one native and two introduced. The black-tailed

Mule Deer

or mule deer are native. They are the smallest of the three species and can be identified easily by their black tail and white rump.

The two non-native deer are the axis deer and fallow deer, both brought to Point Reyes in the 1940s by a sport hunter who got them from the San Francisco Zoo. Fallow deer, native to the Mediterranean region, can be identified by their palmated antlers and variable color, which ranges from white to almost black. Males begin rutting in fall and often engage in vigorous conflict. Antlers are shed in the spring.

Fallow Deer

Axis deer, native to India and the largest of the three species, are best identified by their brown coloring with spotted sides. Male antlers are shed in the summer and regrown each fall. Older bucks carry an eye guard or tine near the antler base. Axis deer are often seen in the open headlands north of Limantour road. They are more wary than the others and keep their distance.

Axis Deer

Both species of non-native deer must be culled to keep their numbers down. Park rangers hunt them each winter in order to maintain a population of around 300 deer.

Smaller Animals

There are dozens of smaller animals living on Point Reyes. Jules Evens, *The Natural History of the Point Reyes Peninsula*, lists over 45 species including possums, shrews, moles, bats, beavers and rats. There are two skunks on Point Reyes, the striped and the spotted skunk. Raccoons are plentiful as campers will attest. Three of the more interesting animals are shown here.

Grey Fox

The grey fox is found in coastal scrub, chaparral and grasslands. It sometimes has a reddish hue on its front flanks and can be best identified by its black-tipped tail.

Bobcats are common on Point Reyes, but probably seen less often than foxes. They can be found in coastal canyons and along the edges of meadows.

Bobcat

The brush rabbit or cottontail is very common and can often be seen along the edges of trails passing through dense coyote bush. Their population is kept in check by foxes, bobcats, weasels, hawks and owls.

Animal Tracks

Brush Rabbit

Most animals are not easily seen. They are wary of open areas and many only appear at dusk or at night. Their footprints are the primary evidence we see during the daytime. The inside back cover shows footprints of some Point Reyes animals.

A9 Sea and Shore Birds

Common Goldeneye 18"
Bucephala clangula

Killdeer 10"
Charadrius vociferus

Willet 15"
Catoptrophorus semipalmatus

Bufflehead 14"
Bucephala albeola

Western Sandpiper 7"
Calidris mauri

American Oystercatcher 16"
Haematopus palliatus

Ruddy Duck 15"
Oxyura jamaicensis

Common Murre 16"
Uria aalge

Species	Spr	Sum	Fall	Wint	General Habitat
Common Goldeneye	2	5	2	2	Lagoons
Bufflehead	2	5	2	1	Lagoons - Ponds
Ruddy Duck	2	5	2	1	Lagoons
Killdeer	2	2	2	2	Grasslands - Ponds - Coastal
Amer. Oystercatcher	4	3	4	4	Coastal
Willet	2	5	1	1	Lagoons - Coastal
Western Sandpiper	1	5	1	1	Lagoons - Ponds
Common Murre	1	1	2	2	Coastal - Ocean
1 = Abundant, 2 = Common, 3 = Fairly Common, 4 = Uncommon, 5 = Rare					

Common Loon 32"
Gavia immer

Western Grebe 25"
*Aechmophorus
occidentalis*

Brown Pelican 50"
Pelecanus occidentalis

Brandt's Cormorant 34"
*Phalaccrocorax
penicillatus*

Great Blue Heron 47"
Ardea herodias

Great Egret 39"
Casmerodius albus

Northern Pintail 27"
Anas acuta

Surf Scoter 19"
Melanitta perspicillata

Species	Spr	Sum	Fall	Wint	General Habitat
Common Loon	3	5	3	1	Lagoons - Coastal
Western Grebe	3	5	3	2	Coastal - Lagoons
Brown Pelican	5	4	2	4	Lagoons - Coastal
Brandt's Cormorant	2	2	2	1	Coastal
Great Blue Heron	3	3	3	3	Lagoons
Great Egret	3	3	3	3	Lagoons
Northern Pintail	3	5	2	1	Lagoons - Ponds
Surf Scoter	2	4	3	1	Ocean - Lagoons - Coastal

1 = Abundant, 2 = Common, 3 = Fairly Common, 4 = Uncommon, 5 = Rare

A10 Land Birds

Turkey Vulture 29"
Cathartes aura

Tree Swallow 5"
Tachycineta bicolor

Allen's Hummingbird 3"
Selasphorus sasin

Scrub Jay 12"
Aphelocoma coerulescens

Red-tailed Hawk 22"
Buteo jamaicensis

Acorn Woodpecker 9"
Melanerpes formicivorus

Pygmy Nuthatch 4"
Sitta pygmaea

California Quail 10"
Callipepla callifornica

Species	Spr	Sum	Fall	Wint	General Habitat
Turkey Vulture	2	2	2	2	Aerial
Red-tailed Hawk	2	2	2	2	Aerial - Scrub- Grasslands
California Quail	1	1	1	1	Scrub
Allen's Hummingbird	2	1	5	5	Streams - Scrub
Acorn Woodpecker	3	3	3	3	Forest - Visitor Center Area
Tree Swallow	2	3	3	5	Ponds - Forest
Scrub Jay	1	1	1	1	Scrub
Pygmy Nuthatch	3	3	3	3	Forest
1 = Abundant, 2 = Common, 3 = Fairly Common, 4 = Uncommon, 5 = Rare					

Wrentit 6"
Chamaea fasciata

**Rufous-sided
Towhee 8"**
Pipilo erythrophthalmus

**Golden-crowned
Sparrow 6"**
Zonotrichia atricapilla

Hutton's Vireo 4"
Vireo huttoni

Tricolored Blackbird 8"
Agelaius tricolor

**White-crowned
Sparrow 6"**
Zonotrichia leucophrys

American Goldfinch 5"
Carduelis tristis

Wilson's Warbler 4"
Wilsonia pusilla

Species	Spr	Sum	Fall	Wint	General Habitat
Wrentit	2	2	2	2	Scrub
Hutton's Vireo	3	3	3	3	Forest - Streams
Wilson's Warbler	2	1	2	5	Streams - Forest
Rufous-sided Towhee	2	1	2	2	Scrub
White-crown Sparrow	2	2	1	1	Scrub
Golden-crown Sparrow	3	5	2	2	Scrub - Grasslands
Tricolored Blackbird	5	5	3	3	Pastures - Ponds
American Goldfinch	2	2	2	5	Grasslands - Scrub
1 = Abundant, 2 = Common, 3 = Fairly Common, 4 = Uncommon, 5 = Rare					

A11 Plant Communities

In his book, *The Natural History of Point Reyes*, Jules Evens states that, "Few areas on the North American landmass host the variety of habitats found within the 100 square miles on the Point Reyes Peninsula." The combination of latitude, climate, geology and topography have made Point Reyes a botanical treasure chest. When you visit Point Reyes, you'll discover four major plant communities, the Douglas fir forest, the Bishop pine forest, the coastal scrub and the grass or pastureland.

Douglas Fir Forest

The Douglas fir forest covers about 20% of the Point Reyes peninsula dominating the moister ridges, canyons and valleys. The Douglas fir is a majestic tree that can reach a height of 250' with a pyramid shaped crown. The one inch needles are sprayed out at various angles and the 2-3 inch cones have a dozen or so small mouse-like tails that clearly distinguish them from other conifers.

Douglas Fir

Elderberry, huckleberry and ferns comprise most of the understory in the Douglas fir forest. You can get a good feel for the forest by hiking any of the trails out of Bear Valley and Five Brooks.

Bishop Pine Forest

Lying due north of the Douglas fir forest, on slightly drier slopes and canyons of Inverness Ridge, the Bishop pine forest covers about 13% of Point Reyes. Bishop pine grow to about 70' in height and are similar in shape to Monterey pines. The needles of the Bishop pine are 2-4 inches long and come two to a bunch. (Monterey pines have slightly longer needles, three to a bunch.) The asymmetrical cones are tight swirls 3-5 inches in size that open to release seeds in hot weather or after fires.

Bishop Pine

Other plants found in the Bishop pine understory include coffeeberry, huckleberry, salal and in drier areas, manzanita and ceanothus.

A good way to practice distinguishing between Douglas fir and Bishop pine is to hike the transition zone between these communities which lies roughly between the Sky and Bayview trailhead. See Hike 17.

Coastal Scrub

The coastal scrub community covers about 15% of the peninsula with 4-6' shrubs that range from impenetrable thickets to isolated shrubs dotting grassy hillsides. The dominant plant is coyote bush, a nondescript shrub that forms white flowers in summer.

Joining the coyote bush in this community are sword fern, bracken fern, coffeeberry, bush lupine, monkeyflower and poison oak. California sagebrush

Coyote Bush

with grey-green needle-like leaves can also be found on drier slopes.

Grass, Prairie and Pastureland

The largest area of Point Reyes, just over 50% is covered with grasses. Historically, much of this land has been used for dairy and cattle grazing and many of the native, perennial bunchgrasses have been replaced with non-native annuals like wild oats.

Other Communities

Several smaller areas on Point Reyes include the salt marsh, freshwater marsh, sand dune and riparian communities.

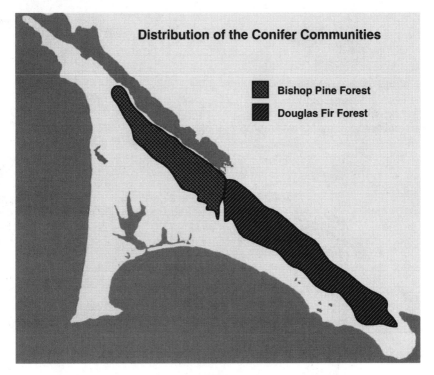

Distribution of the Conifer Communities

Bishop Pine Forest
Douglas Fir Forest

A12 Berries and Ferns

Two favorite groups of plants found on Point Reyes are berries and ferns. Ferns are treasured for their symmetry and delicate shape. Berries provide showy flowers and colorful fruit. All of the species shown below, except the blackberry, thrive in the shady canyons and ridges of the conifer forest where they are kept moist by winter rain and summer fog.

Berries

Berries grow on trees, shrubs, vines and groundcovers and come in a variety of flavors. Some are edible, some slightly toxic and some downright poisonous. An important Berry Rule is,

"Never taste a berry unless you know what it is."

Here are five of the most common berries found on Point Reyes and their suitablility for eating.

Red elderberry, to 15'
White flowers - spring
Red berries may be
toxic.

Thimbleberry, to 8'
White flowers - spring
Red berries in
summer are edible
when soft.

Huckleberry, to 10'
White flowers - spring
Blue berries in fall are
edible.

Red-Flowering
Currant, to 10'
Red flowers - early
spring. Purple berries
are barely edible.

Blackberry, vine to 5'
White flowers - spring
Black berries range
from tart to sweet.

Ferns

Ferns are unusual in that the main part of the fern is a leaf, called a frond. More complex ferns, like the bracken fern, are a classic example of a fractal shape in nature. Fractals maintain similarity as you zoom in on them. Look closely at a bracken fern. The side leaflets are shaped just like the whole leaf. Likewise, the shape is repeated in the subleaflets.

Sword fern, to 5'
Very common

Bracken fern, to 4'
Very common

Lady fern, to 4'
Classic shape

Maidenhair fern, to 1'
Shady banks

Five-finger fern, to 1'
Moist banks

Ferns are different from most plants in that they reproduce by spores rather than flowers and seeds. The life cycle of a fern includes two separate plants: a small, rarely-seen plant called a gametophyte and the sporophyte which we call a fern.

An individual fern can produce hundreds of thousands of spores in small capsules on the underside of each leaflet. After the capsule springs open, the spores are released and if conditions are right, grow into a gametophyte about 1/4" in size with male and female parts. If fertilization occurs, the fertilized egg develops into a new fern.

100

A13 White - Cream Wildflowers

Hairy Star Tulip
Calochortus tolmiei
Plant height: 15 inches
Flower size: 1-2 inches
Leaf length: 5-12 inches
Season: April-July
Habitat: Moist, grassy coastal slopes

Milkmaids
Cardamine californica
Plant height: 16 inches
Flower size: 1/2 inch
Leaf length: 2 inches
Season: January-March
Habitat: Meadows, fields

Morning glory
Convolvulus occidentalis
Plant height: 4-6 feet
Flower size: 1-2 inches
Leaf length: 1 1/2 inches
Season: April-August
Habitat: Coastal scrub, rocky bluffs

Other common white - cream wildflowers are

Fairy Bells ..... Feb-Jul, 2 feet, white, bell-shaped flowers
Zigadene ..... Feb-Apr, 1-2 feet, white flower cluster
Alum-root ..... May-Jul, 2 feet, small white flowers
Yarrow ..... Apr-Sep, 18 inches, fern-like leaves, white flower cluster

Cow Parsnip
Heracleum lanatum
Plant height: 3-9 feet
Flower size: 1/2 -1 inch
Leaf length: 8-15 inches
Season: March-May
Habitat: Coastal scrub, grassland

Slim Solomon
Smilacina stellata var. sessilifolia
Plant height: 1-2 feet
Flower size: 1/4 inch
Leaf length: 2-6 inches
Season: February-April
Habitat: Wooded or brushy hills

Wild Cucumber
Marah fabaceous
Plant height: 10-20 feet
Flower size: 1/2 inch
Leaf length: 2-4 inches
Season: April-July
Habitat: Coastal dunes, coastal scrub

Wallflower
Erysimum concinnum
Plant height: 8-12 inches
Flower size: 1-1 1/2 inches
Leaf length: 1-3 inches
Season: February-July
Habitat: Coastal dunes, rocky bluffs

A14 Yellow - Orange Wildflowers

Buttercup
Ranunculus californicus
Plant height: 8-16 inches
Flower size: 1 inch
Leaf length: 1-1 1/2 inches
Season: February-May
Habitat: Low moist fields, brushy hills

California Poppy
Eschscholzia californica
Plant height: 8-16 inches
Flower size: 1-2 inches
Leaf length: 1-2 inches
Season: March-October
Habitat: Grassy hills, rocky slopes

Lizard Tail
Eriophyllum staechadifolium
Plant height: 1-5 feet
Flower size: 1/2 inch
Leaf length: 1-2 inches
Season: February-July
Habitat: Coastal scrub, coastal strand

Other common yellow - orange wildflowers are

Brass Buttons ..... Mar-Dec, 10 inches, yellow button-like flowers
Gumplant .....Jun-Aug, 1 foot, 2 inch daisy-like flowers
Sun Cups .....Feb-May, 4 inches, early flower, 4 yellow petals
Footsteps of Spring ..... Jan-May, 14 inches, early flower

Gold Fields
Lasthenia californica
Plant height: 8 inches
Flower size: 1 inch
Leaf length: 1/2 -1 inch
Season: March-June
Habitat: Meadows, grassy hills

Bush Monkeyflower
Mimulus aurantiacus
Plant height: 2-5 feet
Flower size: 1 1/2 -2 inches
Leaf length: 1-3 inches
Season: March-August
Habitat: Chaparral

Hairy Cat's Ear
Hypochoeris radicata
Plant height: 2-16 inches
Flower size: 1 inch
Leaf length: 3-6 inches
Season: April-December
Habitat: Widespread

Fiddleneck
Amsinckia intermedia
Plant height: 8 inches - 2 feet
Flower size: 1/2 inch
Leaf length: 1-6 inches
Season: March-June
Habitat: Grassland, ocean bluffs

Buckwheat
Eriogonum latifolium ssp. *nudum*
Plant height: 1-1 1/2 feet
Flower size: 1 inch
Leaf length: 1-2 inches
Season: June-November
Habitat: Rocky bluffs

Checkerbloom
Sidalcea malvaeflora
Plant height: 1-2 feet
Flower size: 1 inch
Leaf length: 1 inch
Season: March-May
Habitat: Open grassy hills

Farewell to Spring
Clarkia purpurea ssp. *quadrivulnera*
Plant height: 6-15 inches
Flower size: 1-1 1/2 inches
Leaf length: 1/2 -2 inches
Season: May-August
Habitat: Brushy or grassy slopes

Other common pink-red wildflowers are

Foxglove .....May-Aug, 3 feet, pink, hanging, bell-shaped flowers
Coyote Mint .....Jun-Sep, 1 foot, mint odor, pink flower heads
Sea Rocket .....May-Nov, 10 inches, succulent leaves, pink flowers
Johnny-tuck .....Mar-May, 6 inches, flower with white, pink and rose

Columbine
Aquilegia formosa
Plant height: 1-2 feet
Flower size: 1 inch
Leaf length: 2 inches
Season: April-June
Habitat: Brushy slopes, moist woods

Indian Paintbrush
Castilleja affinis
Plant height: 1-1 1/2 feet
Flower size: 1/2 -1 inch
Leaf length: 1-3 inches
Season: March-August
Habitat: Coastal scrub, coastal bluffs

Shooting Star
Dodecatheon hendersonii
Plant height: 8-16 inches
Flower size: 1 inch
Leaf length: 2-6 inches
Season: February-April
Habitat: Moist slopes

Sea Pink
Armeria maritima var. *californica*
Plant height: 1 1/2 -2 feet
Flower size: 1/2 inch
Leaf length: 2-6 inches
Season: April-August
Habitat: Coastal scrub, coastal bluffs

A16 Blue - Purple Wildflowers

Blue Dicks
Brodiaea pulchella
Plant height: 1-2 feet
Flower size: 1 inch
Leaf length: 6-16 inches
Season: March-June
Habitat: Open or wooded hills

Blue-eyed Grass
Sisyrinchium bellum
Plant height: 6-18 inches
Flower size: 1/2 -1 inch
Leaf length: 4-24 inches
Season: March-May
Habitat: Open grassy hills

Douglas Iris
Iris douglasiana
Plant height: 6-18 inches
Flower size: 2-3 inches
Leaf length: 6-18 inches
Season: March-May
Habitat: Open grassy hills

Other common blue-purple wildflowers are

Baby Blue Eyes ..... Mar-May, 8 inches, pale-blue, one inch flowers
Sea Lavender ..... Jul-Dec, 18 inches, clusters of lavender flowers
Blue Coast Gilia ..... May-Jul, 1 foot, compact heads of blue flowers
California Phacelia ..... Apr-Jul, 1 foot, coil of lavender flowers

Hound's Tongue
Cynoglossum grande
Plant height: 1-3 feet
Flower size: 1/2 inch
Leaf length: 3-6 inches
Season: February-April
Habitat: Moist woods, brushy slopes

Hedge Nettle
Stachys rigida var. *quercetorum*
Plant height: 1-2 feet
Flower size: 1/2 -1 inch
Leaf length: 2-3 inches
Season: May-August
Habitat: Widespread

Bush Lupine
Lupinus arboreus
Plant height: 3-6 feet
Flower size: 1/2 inch
Leaf length: 1-2 inches
Season: March-August
Habitat: Coastal dunes, coastal scrub

Seaside Daisy
Erigeron glaucus
Plant height: 4-12 inches
Flower size: 1-1 1/2 inches
Leaf length: 4 inches
Season: May-August
Habitat: Coastal bluffs, coastal dunes

A17 Geology of Point Reyes

The theory of plate tectonics suggests that the earth's crustal surface, the upper forty miles, is composed of six major, rigid plates that move on a hot plastic interior. These plates are constantly interacting as new plate material oozes up in some areas, like Iceland, and old plate material disappears in other areas, like the deep sea trenches adjacent to the Aleutian Islands.

One of these plates, the Pacific plate containing Point Reyes, Los Angeles and most of the Pacific Ocean, is moving northwest relative to the North American plate and is slowly disappearing into the Alaskan trench. Although the Pacific plate is moving at an average speed of 1.3" per year, the motion is not steady. For example, where the two plates meet, as they do along the San Andreas and related fault lines, there can be sudden plate motion of up to 20 feet, as in the big San Francisco quake of 1906.

San Andreas Rift Zone

One of the most distinguishing features of the Point Reyes peninsula is the Olema Valley which runs northwesterly along Hwy. 1. This valley, including Tomales Bay, is prime evidence of the San Andreas rift zone, a collection of fault lines that mark the boundary of the North American and Pacific plates.

The Olema Valley offers a striking example of fault topography consisting of sag ponds, streams, small ridges and folded hills created by the uplifting, settling and shifting at the edges of these two great plates. Many of these features can be seen on the Earthquake, Olema Valley and Rift Zone trails.

The rocks to the east of the Olema Valley are a mixture of sandstone, greenstone, chert and serpentine that make up the Franciscan Formation. They are completely different from those of the Point Reyes peninsula which are mostly granite overlaid by marine deposits of sandstone, shale, siltstone, mudstone and greensand.

Granite

Granite is the underlying rock, the bedrock of the Point Reyes peninsula. However, two-thirds of this rock is now covered by layers of marine sediments. The exposed portion of the granite base lies mainly along the Inverness Ridge from Mt. Wittenberg north to Pierce Point. Examples of this mottled rock can be seen at the Visitor's Center and along the Earthquake, Sky and Tomales Point trails.

Marine Deposits

The largest of the marine layers is the Monterey Formation. It is composed of cherts and organic shales deposited and solidified in distinct layers of one to three inches thick. The Monterey Formation can be seen on the coastal cliffs from Duxbury Point to Bolinas Point. Outcroppings near Abbotts Lagoon and Kehoe Beach look like stepping stones, while roadside cuts near the Clem Miller Center appear as contorted slabs.

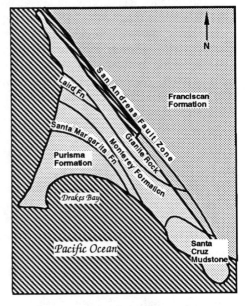

Geology of Point Reyes
Adapted from R. Melander, 1987
Clark, 1984 and Galloway, 1977

The next largest deposit, the Purisma Formation, consists of a softer sediment of muddy deposits. It is lightly colored and contains abundant microscopic fossils and occasional large fossils (collecting is prohibited). While it is not as widespread as the older Monterey shale, it is extensively exposed and easier to see, especially along Drakes Bay.

What is now called Santa Cruz Mudstone was originally thought to be part of the Monterey Formation. However, a fossil seacow discovered near Bolinas by College of Marin students indicated that the rocks were vastly different in age from the Monterey Formation. Subsequent work by the US Geological Survey clarified their origin.

The Pursima Formation and Santa Margarita Formation were thought to be unique to Point Reyes and were originally called the Drakes Bay Formation. Later, the USGS survey discovered that similar deposits existed elsewhere and the area was renamed.

It should be mentioned that topsoil ranging from one-half to three feet deep covers most of the formations mentioned here. These soils are formed by the mixing of the parent material with organic matter, a process that can produce unique soil and plant characteristics.

A18 Weather of Point Reyes

Point Reyes juts out into the Pacific Ocean, a geological, climatogical and vegetative island, riding the Pacific Plate on its northward journey relative to the mainland. Consequently, the weather on Point Reyes is dominated by the ocean. Summers at Point Reyes are cooler, and winters are warmer than areas inland. The difference in average temperature between summer and winter is just four degrees Fahrenheit. Although the temperature is fairly uniform, there are microclimates, significant climate differences that depend on location, terrain and season.

Winter

Winter at Point Reyes, from about mid-November to mid-March, is the rainy season. During this time, the jet stream often drops down over Northern California delivering a series of low pressure storm systems that dump an average of 10 to 60 inches of rain per year, depending on location. The headlands area gets the least rain. The lighthouse averages just 12 inches per year. Bear Valley averages 45 inches of rain per year.

Winter is not all storms, however. Between storms, some of the best coastal weather occurs. Often when much of northern California is socked in with cold, bone-chilling valley fog, Point Reyes basks in warm sunshine. This fog is produced by lack of winds and nighttime radiative cooling. At the coast, the moderating influence of the ocean keeps the temperature above the dew point and no fog develops, allowing the sun to warm Point Reyes from dawn to dusk.

Winter provides great hiking time, especially along the coast. Here, you find ocean waves crashing, grey whales migrating south, seals basking on the beaches, birds wintering in the marshes and lagoons, and in February, the first iris blooming on south-facing hills.

Spring

Spring is a time of transition. The weather is often unpredictable. Usually, by the middle of spring, northwest winds begin to establish a pattern which leads to either clear and windy, or foggy and windy, days. Occasionally, especially during El Nino years, the jet stream remains south keeping March and April wet and unsettled.

Some things are predictable in spring. Each April, the headlands, pasturelands and hills produce a glorious carpet of green, dotted with magnificent wildflowers. If the weather cooperates, spring can be the most exhilarating time to hike. It can also be a time for to watch for returning whales and migrating birds.

Summer

Summer at Point Reyes, especially the headlands, can be cold, foggy windy and uncomfortable. The chaplain on Drake's expedition, Francis Fletcher, described it this way, "nipping colds as we have never seen before" and " thick mists and the most stinking fog". This was in June, 1579!

An interesting side note of the summer fog is that the entrance to San Francisco Bay was missed by European explorers for almost 200 years. It was not until 1769, that the Spanish explorer, Captain Gaspar de Portola, traveling by land, found this great natural harbor. Had the explorers sailed the coast in winter, they surely would have found the bay, but then they would have experienced the wrath of winter storms.

Why is the summer so inhospitable? The answer lies in the Pacific High, a high pressure system that forms off the California coast. This high produces northwest winds that create a surface current in the ocean that moves south. Because the earth rotates, any object that moves towards the equator, away from the axis of rotation, falls behind the earth's surface. In the northern hemisphere, southward moving objects like airplanes, winds and seas veer to the right. In the ocean, the south moving surface current moves west, causing an upwelling of cold water along the coast. When warm, moisture-laden air gets close to the cold upwelled water, fog forms. On a typical summer day, this ocean fog will be sucked inland in the afternoon by hot air rising in the interior valleys. Later, the next day, the fog will burn off to the ocean. This cycle repeats itself with surprising regularity.

Fall

Like spring, fall is a period of transition. If the summer high stays in place, the winds and fog remain. However, once the Pacific High moves out of position, the upwelling ceases and Point Reyes experiences its warmest weather. Because the hills are dry and brown, the best way to enjoy this weather is to hike the coast, visit the beaches and explore tidepools.

Other changes also occur in fall. Willows, alders and buckeyes lose their leaves. Poison oak and blackberry shrubs provide red color and the big leaf maple turns yellow. Migrant and wintering birds begin to arrive and the first storms freshen the air.

A19 History of Point Reyes

Four hundred years ago, the population of the Point Reyes peninsula was greater than it is today! The late historian, Jack Mason, claims that there were 113 village sites, mostly located around Tomales Bay, Drakes Estero and other seashore areas. These Native Americans were Coast Miwoks, described by Francis Fletcher, chaplain on Drake's expedition, as "a people of a tractable, free and loving nature, without guile or treachery."

The Miwoks had a rich variety of food at Point Reyes. They hunted small game, deer and elk, gathered acorns and berries and enjoyed the bounty of the sea - clams, mussels and fish. You can get some idea about how they lived by visiting Kule Loklo, a model village constructed in 1976 near park headquarters.

What happened to the Miwoks? The early 1800s were a disaster for them. Most of the Miwoks were persuaded to join the mission at San Rafael soon after it was established in 1817. Here, they took up agriculture and were to be baptized and civilized. The intentions of the missionaries may have been good, but the experiment failed. Disease, abuse and disenchantment with western ways set in. Shortly after secularizion of the missions in 1834 by the Mexican government, a period of confrontation developed. When it was over in the late 1800s, the remaining Miwoks of Point Reyes scattered to the north.

Sir Francis Drake

Forty-one years before the landing of the Mayflower on Plymouth Rock, the English captain, Francis Drake, careened his sailing ship, the Golden Hind, on the soft sands at Drakes Estero. For 36 days, Drake worked to repair and replenish his ship before returning to England.

How do we know Drake landed at Point Reyes? Although there are an assortment of claims for other landing sites, such as Tomales Bay, Bolinas Lagoon, Bodega Bay and the Tiburon Peninsula, the overwhelming conclusion by

Artists Conception of Drake Landing the Golden Hind

historians here and in England is that Drake landed at Point Reyes. Their evidence includes:

- the description of the landing site as "white banks and cliffs", like those in England, which matches Drakes Bay better than anywhere else.
- the description of the weather as "nipping colds and stinking fogs" where they didn't see the sun or stars for 14 days.
- the reference to offshore islands which would be the Farallones.
- the map of New Albion made twelve years later by a Dutch cartographer that can be made to fit Drakes Estero.
- the description of meetings with local Native Americans.

A brass plate left behind by Drake and supposedly found near San Quentin in 1936 has been the subject of much controversy. It is now believed to be a prank.

Shipwrecks and the Coast Guard

The second European to set foot on Point Reyes suffered the ignoble site of seeing his ship wrecked at almost the exact spot of Drake's landing 16 years earlier. Sebastian Cermeno, sailing out of Acapulco, had arrived along the coast by way of Manila. His ship, the San Agustin, loaded with goods from the Orient, was battered and leaky after an arduous Pacific journey. In early November of 1595, a storm churned up southerly waves that ripped the San Agustin from its anchorage and drove her onto the beach where she was destroyed by pounding breakers.

Cermeno and 70 men set out in a small launch for Acapulco, leaving behind the San Agustin and its treasures. Three hundred and fifty years later, archeologists probing Miwok ruins in Drakes Bay, unearthed more than 100 fragments of Chinese porcelain identified as coming from the Wan Li period of the late 1500s. (Some historians argue that the porcelain actually came from the Drake expedition.)

The naval historian, Don Marshall, suggests that the Spaniard Cermeno found Drake's brass plate claiming New Albion for England and recorded the fact in his log. He reaches this conclusion by observing that Cermeno was a meticulus logkeeper, yet the entries surrounding his ships disappearance are almost non-existent. It seemed as though pages had been removed from the log.

Cermeno's shipwreck was the first of over fifty recorded shipwrecks along the Point Reyes peninsula. In 1841, the French trader Jose Yves Limantour, became stranded at what is now known as Limantour Spit. In 1861, a clippership sailed "fearlessly to her doom on Point Reyes beach with all sails set" according to Jack Mason.

By 1852, the large number of shipwrecks prompted Congress to appropriate $25,000 for a lighthouse. After 18 years of negotiation and construction, the lighthouse finally went into service 294 feet above sea level, yet 300 feet below the towering clifftop. Unfortunately, the light and its foghorn did not end shipwrecks. A Lifesaving Station was built in 1890 on Point Reyes Beach where it operated until 1927, when it was moved to Drakes Bay.

One of the most dramatic rescues took place in 1913 when the lumber schooner Samoa ran aground along the great beach. With spilled lumber thrashing in the surf, the lifesaving

The Wreck of the Somoa, 1913.

crew rigged a breeches buoy and safely removed everyone on board, one of the greatest breeches buoy rescues in U.S. history.

Dividing Up The Land

Between 1769 and 1823, Spain established 21 missions throughout California to solidify its presence and colonize the local population. When Mexico overthrew Spanish rule in 1822, they used the Mexican Land Grant to establish control. The great ranchos created by these grants were one of the most important influences in California history, as they concentrated land ownership in the hands of a select few.

During this time, Point Reyes was divided into two parcels: a 35,000 acre grant to John Berry, a colonel in the Mexican army and a 9,000 acre grant to Rafael Garcia, a corporal, once stationed at Yerba Buena. However, these grants contained vague conditions and overlapping boundaries, which left a heritage of confused land ownership. Speculators, sales, bad debts and land grabbers added to the confusion and when the dust settled in the late 1850s, Garcia and three gentlemen from Vermont owned most of the land. Their names,

Home Ranch, circa 1910

Oscar Shafter, James Shafter and Charles Howard would remain connected to Point Reyes up until World War II.

During the first half of the 20th century, Point Reyes was a rural area that supported cattle and dairy ranches, fishing and occasional hunters and vacationers. However, by the late 1950s, Point Reyes was on the verge of a major transition. A freeway was planned to connect Hwy. 101 to West Marin. A lumber mill was clearcutting Inverness Ridge. Developers were subdividing Limantour Beach and Lake Ranch. Hundreds of lots were available. Eighteen houses were built and sold. A marina and harbor were planned for Bolinas Lagoon. A large campground was planned on park land at Bear Valley. Shopping centers and new roads were being proposed to meet the new growth.

Creating a Park

Although there had been interest in creating a national park at Point Reyes as early as 1935, it was not until 1959 that Congress was persuaded to appropriate $15,000 to study the idea. Later that year, Congressman Clem Miller introduced legislation to acquire land.

This legislation intensified the political battle. How big would the park be? Developers continued to build, expecting that a park would increase land values. The ranchers were nervous and afraid of losing their land or prospects for profit. For three years, the debate raged. Congressman toured the area. Fortunately, the weather cooperated at key times and everyone agreed that Point Reyes was a special place worth saving.

Legislation creating the seashore was enacted and signed into law by President Kennedy in 1962. The park was to include 53,000 acres. A compromise was reached with the ranchers. It was agreed that 26,000 acres would remain the property of the current ranch owners. If they wanted to sell, the government would have the option to buy.

Although Congress voted to create a park, they didn't appropriate enough money to buy the land. By 1970, another crisis was brewing. It took a superhuman, grassroots effort by the Save Our Seashore committee to gather over 500,000 signatures and persuade Congress to appropriate sufficient funds to buy the remaining land.

The delay in completing the park had one unforeseen benefit. Originally, park planners hoped to make the park accessible for recreation, such as boating and camping. New and improved roads were planned. Later, in 1969, a new type of park was conceived. Much of the seashore was to be conserved as a wilderness. In 1976, 32,000 acres were designated the Philip Burton Wilderness Area, where no vehicles or man-made structures are allowed.

The early park conservationists have left us a wonderful legacy. Even though over two million people visit and use Point Reyes annually, it only takes a half-hour hike to get into the wilderness and enjoy the grandeur and solitude of this remarkable peninsula.

A20 Local Resources

In the early 1960s, the Marin County Master Plan proposed a freeway from Highway 101 to West Marin, either along Sir Francis Drake Blvd. or along some new corridor. If this had happened, you would find many more accomodations and amenities near Point Reyes than you will today.
However, the area is not totally inhospitable, and what you find is usually of high quality. Here is a partial list of the major lodging, food and other resources. Please call to verify hours and services. All numbers are in the 415 area code.

Point Reyes National Seashore
First-time visitors should stop at the main Visitor Center at Bear Valley to view exhibits and pick up information about a wide variety of ranger-led activities and hikes.

464-5100

Bear Valley Visitor Center: 663-1092. Main Visitor Center.
Lighthouse Visitor Center: 669-1534. Check hours.
Drakes Beach Visitor Center: 669-1250. A cafe is located here.
Hostel information: 663-8811 early morning and evenings only.
Backpacking Reservations - call the Bear Valley Visitor Center.
Recorded Weather and Whale Information: 663-9029

Point Reyes Station
Inns of Point Reyes - referral for several small inns: 663-1420
Seashore B&B's of Marin - referral service: 663-9373
West Marin Vacation Rentals - vacation homes: 1-800-540-1776
Station House Cafe: 663-1515
Chez Madeleine: 663-9177
Mike's Cafe: 663-1536
Bovine Bakery: 663-9420

Inverness and Inverness Park
Golden Hinde Inn and Marina - 35 rooms: 1-800-339-9398
Barnaby's By The Bay Restaurant: 669-1114
Inverness Valley Inn - 11 rooms: 669-7250
Inverness Motel - 7 rooms: 669-1081
Knave of Hearts Bakery: 663-1236
Grey Whale Pizza: 669-1244
Vladimiir's Restaurant: 669-1021
Manka's Czech Restaurant: 669-1034
Perry's Deli: 663-1491

Olema
Point Reyes Seashore Lodge - 18 rooms, 3 suites: 663-9000
Olema Farm House - Restaurant and Bar: 663-1264
Olema Ranch Campground - 32 acres - hookups: 1-800-655-2267
Olema Inn and Restaurant - 6 rooms: 663-9559

Bolinas
Bolinas Bay Bakery and Cafe: 868-0211
Blue Heron Inn and Restaurant - 2 rooms: 868-1102

Stinson Beach
Ocean Court Motel - 5 rooms: 868-0212
Sandpiper Motel - 5 rooms: 868-1632
Stinson Beach Motel - 6 rooms: 868-1712
The Sand Dollar Restaurant: 868-0434
Stinson Beach Grill: 868-2002

Rentals
Horses at Five Brooks Stables: 663-1570
Bicycles at Point Reyes Pro Cyclery: 663-1046
Bicycles at Olema Trailhead Rental: 663-1958

Education
Point Reyes Field Seminars: Call 663-1200 for a free schedule.
Point Reyes Bird Observatory: 868-1221

Gas Stations
Gas stations are located in Inverness, Point Reyes Station and the
campground at Olema. All are closed by 8 pm.

General Stores
General stores are located in Olema, Inverness, Inverness Park,
Point Reyes Station, Bolinas and Stinson Beach.

Oyster Company
Johnson's Oyster Company - Sir Francis Drake Hwy: 669-1149

Campgrounds
In addition to those listed above, campgrounds are located at Pan
Toll, Mt. Tamalpais and Samuel P.Taylor State Parks.

Medical Services
West Marin Medical Center: 663-1082
Point Reyes Clinic: 663-8666

Emergency
Dial 911

A21 Bibliography

Arnot, Phil. *Point Reyes: Secret Places and Magic Moments.* Wide World Publishing, 1987.

Bakker, Elna. *An Island Called California.* University of California Press, 1971.

Beck, Warren A. and Haase, Ynez D. *Historical Atlas of California.* University of Oklahoma Press, 1974.

Burt, William and Grossenheider, Richard. *Mammals.* Peterson Field Guides, 1980.

Cobb, Boughton. *Ferns.* Peterson Field Guides, 1956.

Evens, Jules G. *The Natural History of the Point Reyes Peninsula.* Point Reyes National Seashore Association, 1988.

Gilliam, Harold. *Island in Time.* Sierra Club, 1962.

Gilliam, Harold. *Weather of the San Francisco Bay Region.* University of California Press, 1962.

Hart, John. *Wilderness Next Door.* Presidio Press, 1979.

Jenkins, Olaf P., ed., *Geologic Guidebook of the San Francisco Bay Counties.* Department of Natural Resources, California, 1951.

Keator, Glenn and Heady, Ruth. *Pacific Coast Fern Finder.* Nature Study Guide, 1981.

Marshall, Don B. *California Shipwrecks.* Superior Publishing Company, 1978.

Mason, Jack. *Point Reyes: The Solemn Land.* North Shore Books, 1970.

Molenaar, Dee. *Point Reyes National Seashore: Pictorial Landform Map.* Wilderness Press, 1988.

Murie, Olaus. *A Field Guide to Animal Tracks.* Houghton Mifflin Company, 1954.

Parsons, Mary Elizabeth. *The Wild Flowers of California.* California Academy of Sciences, 1960.

Peterson, Roger Tory. *A Field Guide to Western Birds.* Houghton Mifflin Company, 1961.

Teather, Louise. *Place Names of Marin.* Scottwall Associates, 1986.

Von der Porten, Edward P. *Drake - Cermeno: An Analysis of Artifacts.* Drake Navigators Guild, 1965.

About the Authors

Kay Martin has a masters degree in botany from San Francisco State University. She works part-time at the California Academy of Sciences and is a volunteer docent for Bay Shore Studies. She is active with the California Native Plant Society.

Don Martin teaches physics and computer science at College of Marin. He has written the study guide, *How to be a Successful Student* and co-authored four computer books, including, *Unix Primer Plus.* The Martins have also written the book, *Mt Tam: A Hiking, Running and Nature Guide.*

The Martins are members of the Sierra Club, Audubon Society and the Tamalpa Running Club. They have four grown children.

Bob Johnson is a well-known Marin County illustrator and designer. He has illustrated over thirty plant books, twenty computer books and a variety of other books, posters and artwork.

Order Form

Books may be ordered from your local bookstore or directly from the publisher at the address below.

Martin Press
PO Box 2109
San Anselmo, CA 94979

The price for direct ordering from the publisher is:

1-3 copies at $9.95 each.

3 or more copies at $8.95 each.

Please include $2.50 per book to cover shipping and tax.

Also available from Martin Press

MT TAM: A Hiking, Running and Nature Guide, 1986

This book describes 32 round trip hikes on Mt. Tam. It covers over 200 miles of trails making up Mt. Tamalpais State Park, Muir Woods and the Marin Municipal Water District. The price is $8.95 plus tax and shipping.